FAITH CLINIC

VOLUME XXXI

-BITTERNESS EDITION-

Dear God, It's Not Me, It's Them, The Gospel According To The Offended

DR. PATRICIA S. TANNER

Published by I.B.G. Publications, Inc., a Power to Wealth Company

Web address: www.ibgpublications.com

admin@ibgpublications.com / 904-419-9810

Copyright, 2026 by Patricia S. Tanner

IBG Publications, Inc., Jacksonville, FL

ISBN: 978-1-971850-19-1

Tanner, Patricia S.
Faith Clinic, Volume XXXI- Bitter Edition- *Dear God, It's Not Me, It's Them, The Gospel According to the Offended*

Printed in the United States of America.

DEDICATION

To the quiet ones who learned to shrink before they ever learned to speak.

To the thoughtful souls who feel deeply, think carefully, and love God fiercely, but often wonder if there is room for them in a world that rewards noise.

This book is dedicated to every person who was told they were "too quiet," too sensitive, too reserved and slowly began believing that presence required performance.

May you discover that you were never meant to become louder, only freer. May you find the courage to be seen without losing the beauty of who you are. And may you finally understand that your quiet was never the problem, fear was.

With compassion and conviction,

DR. PATRICIA S. TANNER
The Faith Doctor

ACKNOWLEDGMENTS

To my Great Physician, Dr. Jesus, thank You for writing every chapter before I lived it. For refusing to let me self-diagnose my pain or medicate my pride. For calling me back when I mistook control for courage, and independence for identity.

To the Holy Spirit, my Counselor and Care Partner, thank You for every whisper, every nudge, every quiet correction that shaped these pages into healing. You are the steady voice in my chaos.

To my family, thank you for loving me through every rewrite, every late night, and every emotional ICU moment of this book's creation. You are my first ministry and my forever reminder that healing is a group project.

To every reader who's ever walked through their own faith rehab, thank you for showing up to your own recovery. You are proof that God still specializes in stubborn patients.

And finally, to every woman and man who's ever looked in the mirror and said, "I shouldn't still be here"… You're right, but grace decided otherwise.

TABLE OF CONTENTS

⚕ FAITH CLINIC INTAKE FORM

(Please complete honestly, denial only delays discharge.)

Patient Name: _______________________________

Date of Admission: _____________________________

Primary Symptom: Unforgiveness disguised as spiritual maturity.
Secondary Symptoms: Selective amnesia, holy side-eyes, compulsive memory of offenses, and recurring "they don't deserve it" syndrome.

Known Triggers: Family reunions, old text messages, passive-aggressive Facebook posts, and childhood flashbacks that still smell like disappointment.

Spiritual History:
☐ Baptized. ☐ Bitter. ☐ Both.

Previous Treatment Attempts:
☐ Ignoring it.
☐ Pretending you're "over it."
☐ Posting a scripture with shade.
☐ Praying but still rolling your eyes.
☐ Telling God it's not unforgiveness, it's boundaries.

Emergency Contact: Jesus Christ, who's been trying to reach you about your heart's extended warranty.

Chief Complaint:" I said I forgave them, but every time I see their name, my blood pressure rises."

✐ WELCOME TO THE CLINIC

Let's be honest, you didn't walk into this clinic by choice. You were dragged here by a Spirit who's tired of watching you treat bitterness like a comfort pet. Maybe you came because your parents never apologized. Maybe your child said something that sliced your heart open. Maybe you're exhausted from being the strong one, the forgiving one, the "bigger person" and now you're quietly simmering under a smile that fools everyone but God.

Bitterness is the silent infection of the soul. It doesn't scream; it simmers. It doesn't always show up in your worship; it hides in your sighs. It sits politely in church, nodding during sermons about forgiveness while internally drafting speeches for people who still "owe you closure." It's spiritual inflammation, the body of Christ's version of emotional arthritis, making movement painful and praise stiff.

Here in the Faith Clinic, we don't sugar-coat spiritual sickness. We identify symptoms and apply truth like disinfectants: it stings before it heals. You'll see that bitterness is not just about what they did, it's about what you let stay infected after the wound.

And yes, this edition cuts deep into **parenthood**, because that's where bitterness often breeds in silence. Some of you are parenting from your own pain, punishing your kids for what your parents never gave you. Others are adult children who still talk to God like He's supposed to re-parent the parent who broke you. This clinic exposes the cycle, how resentment becomes inheritance if not interrupted by grace.

You'll recognize yourself in these pages. The tone might sting, but the treatment plan is divine: **truth, tears, and transformation.** Each chapter walks you through the anatomy of bitterness, the emotional limp, the generational inheritance, the myth of closure, and the hard work of forgiving people who aren't even sorry.

🔧 CLINIC POLICIES

- **No spiritual pretending.** If you're still mad, say so. God already knows.

- **No religious jargon.** Bitterness doesn't respond to clichés; it responds to confession

- **No comparison charts.** Your pain doesn't become smaller because someone else's looks bigger.

- **Confidentiality clause:** What you don't release will eventually reveal itself in your relationships.

- **Side effects may include** peace, joy, emotional clarity, and the sudden urge to apologize first

🧠 DIAGNOSIS

Condition: Chronic Offense with Underlying Unforgiveness Disorder.

Cause: Unprocessed hurt, spiritual pride, and delayed honesty. **Complications:** Relationship decay, generational repetition, and spiritual exhaustion.

Prognosis: 100% recoverable, with obedience, humility, and daily doses of grace.

🧠 DOCTOR'S NOTE

Bitterness doesn't always look evil. Sometimes it looks like "strong boundaries." Sometimes it sounds like "I'm just protecting my peace." But beneath the trendy phrases, there IS a heart that stopped trusting God to handle justice. The cure starts when you admit you've been your own defense attorney for too long.

This clinic isn't about blame, it's about biopsy. We're cutting open the layers of offense to find the infection of unbelief that says, *"If I let this go, I'll lose control."* But newsflash: you never had control. What you have is choice, to heal or to harden. So, breathe. You're not here to be ashamed. You're here to be seen.

⬥ SPIRITUAL VITAL SIGNS CHECK

Test	Healthy Range	Your Reading
Forgiveness Reflex	Responds quickly without emotional delay	☐ Pending
Empathy Levels	Sees pain beyond self	☐ Critically low
Faith Pressure	Trust in God's justice	☐ Fluctuating
Emotional Temperature	Warm, responsive, honest	☐ Lukewarm
Heart Rate	Beating for grace, not revenge	☐ Needs monitoring

⬥ PRESCRIPTION PLAN

- **Daily Dose:** Luke 6:27–28, *"Love your enemies, do good to those who hate you."*

- **Weekly Therapy:** Write letters you'll never send, then pray for them instead of posting them.
- **Monthly Maintenance:** Attend forgiveness follow-ups, not for them, but for your freedom.

- **Emergency Medication:** Psalm 51:10 *"Create in me a clean heart, O God."*

REFLECTION PROMPT

"Who am I still silently punishing, and what is it costing me?" Write their name. Then write yours beside it, because bitterness always chains both people.

DR. PATRICIA S. TANNER

PERSONAL NOTES

INTRODUCTION

Let's be honest, you didn't pick up this book by accident. Something (or someone) pushed a button deep enough that your halo tilted, your patience expired, and now you're trying to convince God it's *their fault*. Don't worry, you're in good company. Welcome to the Gospel According to the Offended, where every believer swears, they're healed until the wrong person walks into the room.

This isn't your typical "how to forgive" devotional written by someone who's never actually had to. This is a field guide for the spiritually exhausted, emotionally over it, church-trained saints who know the right scriptures but still secretly want a few people to *trip just enough to humble them.* We're talking about that quiet grudge that dresses in prayer language, the one that says, "I'm not bitter, I'm just protecting my peace." Sure, Jan.

If you've ever replayed a conversation in your head twenty-seven times and still didn't come out the hero, congratulations, bitterness may have taken out a lease in your heart. And if you've been telling yourself, "It's fine, I've moved on," while still side-eyeing their name in your notifications, this book is the intervention you didn't ask for but absolutely need.

I wrote this because I've been there, trying to heal while still hoping karma runs on divine schedule. I've prayed through clenched teeth, worshiped with crossed arms, and smiled through sermons that felt like personal attacks. And after one too many emotional relapses, I realized something: bitterness doesn't die quietly. It hides, mutates, and then shows up disguised as "discernment," "boundaries," or my personal favorite, "just being real." So, here is the deal, I built this book like a clinic because that's exactly what it feels like: messy, invasive, and a little uncomfortable. Bitterness is a spiritual infection that doesn't heal with denial. It needs truth, tears, and the kind of Holy Ghost surgery that doesn't use anesthesia. You'll squirm. You'll roll your eyes. You'll want to skip chapters. But if you stay on the table, I promise, God knows exactly where the root is buried.

This edition isn't for people who want to *look* forgiving. It's for those who are tired of carrying family resentment, ministry disappointments, and parental guilt like emotional trophies. It's for parents still haunted by how they were raised, children still angry at who didn't show up, and believers who can't figure out why peace keeps dodging them.

So, if you're ready to stop narrating your pain like a testimony and let God disinfect it, welcome to the clinic. It's okay to admit it's not just "them." Sometimes, it's you too. Now grab your chart, breathe deep, and don't flinch when conviction hits, because this time, healings not optional.

Chapter 1:
"I'm Fine" The Emotional Limp You've Normalized

⬤ SYMPTOM: "I'm fine."

You say it like its punctuation, a full stop to any conversation that might dig too deep. The phrase has become your emotional armor, your favorite costume for public survival. You've worn "I'm fine" so long it's practically embroidered on your church lanyard. You've said it in hospital waiting rooms, at the dinner table, in ministry meetings, and even in the mirror, rehearsing it until it sounds convincing enough to silence concern. But let's be real: "I'm fine" is Christian for *"I'm not okay, but I don't trust anyone enough to say it."*

You tell yourself you've moved on, but your conversations still orbit the person who hurt you. You say you're at peace, but your tone sharpens every time someone brings them up. You're not fine; you're functional, and bitterness loves high-functioning people because they're too busy performing stability to notice spiritual decay.

You've built your own emotional triage. You patch yourself with distractions and call it deliverance. You quote scriptures you no longer feel and call it faith. You serve others to avoid sitting still long enough to feel your own emptiness. And when someone tries to ask how you're *really* doing, you hand them your rehearsed smile like a prescription sample: "I'm fine. God is good."

Bitterness has a way of blending in with maturity. It dresses up as independence, sounds like confidence, and moves like "I've just learned to protect my peace." But the truth? You didn't protect your peace; you buried it under walls made of old offenses and unspoken goodbyes.

You've become fluent in emotional avoidance. You know how to talk about pain without ever *feeling* it. You've built altars to "moving on" but secretly left your heart on life support. And when you finally get triggered oh, you call it "discernment." You think you're spiritually sensitive when really, you're emotionally infected. Everything feels personal because your wound hasn't closed. You call it spiritual warfare, but sometimes it's just your bitterness staging a protest.

Now let's take this "I'm fine" act home for a second, because bitterness doesn't clock out when you walk through your front door. It seeps into your parenting, your tone, your patience. You tell your kids, "I'm not mad, I'm disappointed," when really, you're reliving every moment you felt unseen by your own parents. You scold them harder than necessary, not because they deserved it, but because they triggered a memory you never healed from. You keep telling them to "let things go" when you're still carrying decades of your own emotional luggage. "I'm fine" becomes the anthem of your home. Everyone walks on eggshells while pretending everything's normal.

You silence the tension with chores, busy schedules, and perfectly curated family photos. You think you've hidden the limp, but your children can hear it in your tone. They can feel it in your silence. They can sense it in the way you flinch at affection. 

Bitterness is contagious. It doesn't need your permission to spread, just your silence. You can raise grateful kids while still transferring a legacy of unhealed pain if you never model forgiveness in front of them. And then there's church, the breeding ground for polite pain. You shake hands, serve coffee, sing harmonies, but deep down you're tired. You're showing up out of duty, not devotion. You call it "being faithful," but it's more like spiritual muscle memory. You've learned to smile through sermons about forgiveness because admitting you're still angry feels too embarrassing for someone "as mature as you."

Let's not even talk about your prayer life. You've prayed for healing, yes, but mostly for *them* to get what they deserve. You've slipped bitterness into your intercessions and dressed it in holy language: "Lord, expose their hearts."Lord, teach them humility. " "Lord, give them what they've sown." And God, patient as ever, just whispers back, "I'm trying to do that with *you*."

Your limp shows up in your patience level, your sarcasm, your tone when you say "I'm over it" but still manage to mention it in every testimony. It shows up when you serve people with a smile but secretly hope they notice how much you've done for them. It shows up when you talk to God about how much you've forgiven, as if it is a competition He owes you points for.

The emotional limp isn't always loud. Sometimes it's subtle, like the way you avoid certain people at gatherings. Or how your heart rate spikes when you see their name on social media. Or how you smile while scrolling, but your spirit is muttering, "I'm fine. Totally fine. Not bitter. Nope."

The limp grows heavy in silence. Every time you suppress the ache, the bitterness digs deeper roots. Every "I'm fine" waters the soil of resentment until your heart grows hard enough to resist conviction. You stop hearing God clearly, not because He stopped speaking, but because His voice started sounding too much like forgiveness, and you didn't want to go there yet.

Here is the harsh truth: Bitterness doesn't always shout. Sometimes it worships. Sometimes it preaches. Sometimes it hugs people on Sunday mornings and posts verses about peace on Instagram. It knows how to blend in. It wears holiness like a hoodie. But underneath it all, the limp is still there.

You've normalized walking with pain because it's easier than sitting still long enough to heal. You've convinced yourself that numbness equals peace, that silence equals forgiveness, and that distance equals maturity. But God didn't call you to *function* through your limp, He called you to face it. And if you're brave enough to admit that "I'm fine" is a lie, then you're finally ready for treatment. Because in this clinic, pretending is not part of the recovery plan.

⚕ TEACHING

Let's get brutally honest: bitterness rarely enters loudly; it creeps in quietly, usually right after disappointment. Someone you trusted didn't come through. A parent withheld affection. A friend chose silence over explanation. You told yourself, *"It's okay, I'll just move on,"* but you didn't move; you just dragged the wound along for the ride.

The emotional limp shows up in small ways. You overreact to small offenses because old ones never healed. You preach grace but practice distance. You're allergic to vulnerability because the last time you opened, someone weaponized your honesty. You tell people, "I don't need closure," but your sleep schedule disagrees.

Bitterness is a sneaky architect; it builds walls out of memories and calls them boundaries. Before long, you're living in a fortress of self-protection, peeking out the window of "I'm fine" while wondering why peace never visits anymore.

Spiritually, that limp turns into imbalance. You worship, but it's half-hearted. You pray, but it's filtered through suspicion. You serve, but you secretly judge the people you serve beside. Because when the heart stays offended, even obedience feels heavy.

Scripture says in **Hebrews 12:15 (NIV)**: "See to it that no one falls short of the grace of God and that no bitter root grows up to cause trouble and defile many." Notice that *a bitter root grows*. It doesn't appear overnight; it grows underneath politeness and productivity. You can be a loving parent and still resentment model. You can quote Ephesians and still silently despise your father. You can raise children who inherit your faith but also your frustration. Bitterness doesn't skip generations; it mutates until someone finally names it. And naming it is the first step to healing. You can't fix what you refuse to diagnose. The Holy Spirit doesn't perform surgery on what you keep labeling as "just personality." That coldness? That sarcasm? That needs to be right in every argument. Those are defense mechanisms, not fruits of the Spirit.

Let's talk about parenthood for a second. The emotional limp often shows up in how you raise or respond to your kids. You overcorrect because no one corrected you in love. You withdraw because being emotionally present feels dangerous. Or maybe you silently compete with your children's joy because you never experienced your own. Bitterness isn't always rage, sometimes it's quite detachment disguised as discipline. Biblically, think about King Saul. Once anointed, later insecure. His jealousy of David wasn't random; it was unhealed rejection fermenting into bitterness. Saul's limp wasn't physical; it was emotional envy parading as leadership.

Every time David succeeded, Saul's unhealed heart interpreted it as an attack. That's what bitterness distorts perception. You start reading betrayal into blessings. And yet, God doesn't shame Saul for his limp, He exposes it through contrast. The same way He'll use your child's laughter, your friend's forgiveness, or your coworker's peace to remind you what you've lost under the weight of "I'm fine." Conviction isn't cruelty; it's a mirror. God's trying to show you where you've been limping so long you started calling it "my walk."

Let's talk about what it means to walk with a limp. A limp isn't the same as pain. Pain demands attention: a limp adapts to it. Pain says, "Something's wrong." A limp says, "Something's wrong, but I've learned how to hide it." And that's where most believers live, walking through life like emotional gymnasts, adjusting posture, tone, and vocabulary so no one notices the ache underneath their "hallelujah."

The problem is that limps become lifestyles. You've been compensating for so long that your dysfunction feels normal. You've built entire coping mechanisms around your limp, sarcasm, silence, control, emotional distance, passive aggressive "I'm praying for you" texts, all so you never have to admit you're still bleeding. You've even made it spiritual. You tell yourself, *"God's just teaching me patience,"* when really, you're just bitter and tired.

Bitterness is like inflammation of the soul. It's invisible, but it affects everything. It tightens your responses, stiffens your trust, and makes relationships painful. You can't receive love without analyzing it. You can't accept corrections without defending yourself. You can't celebrate others without secretly comparing. It's not because you're evil, it's because the limp won't let you move freely anymore.

The Bitterness Illusion: Strength Vs. Survival

We've glamorized survival. Somewhere along the way, "I'm strong" replaced "I'm healed." We equate endurance with deliverance, forgetting that functioning through trauma is not the same as freedom from it. You can shout in church and still be emotionally paralyzed. You can lead worship with resentment in your veins. You can preach about forgiveness and still fantasize about people "getting what they deserve." You call it discernment. Heaven calls it delay.

Bitterness clouds your spiritual vision. You stop seeing people through grace and start seeing them through your history with pain. Every new person is filtered through your old wound. That's why relationships crumble before they begin, you're not meeting new people; you're re-meeting old offenses wearing new faces. And before you know it, the limp becomes your ministry.

You start serving through pain instead of healing from it. You pour out while running on fumes. You give, not because you're overflowing, but because you're afraid that stopping will make you feel empty again. You've turned service into sedation, if you're busy, you don't have to face yourself.

But here's the issue: unhealed people eventually weaponize serving. You start giving with invisible expectations. You want applause for surviving, validation for enduring, and when it doesn't come, you feel used to it. That's the bitter cycle, giving what you hope someone else will finally notice you for.

Jesus didn't model that. He didn't serve out of scarcity; He served from fullness. The reason He could wash Judas' feet, yes, *Judas* was because His identity wasn't limping. He wasn't triggered by rejection; He was anchored in obedience. That's the goal here, not to stop serving, not to stop loving, but to stop limping while doing it.

The Family Factor, How Bitterness Becomes Inherited

Bitterness doesn't always begin with you. Sometimes it's passed down like family tradition. You watched your parents hold grudges and call it strength. You heard arguments wrapped in Bible verses. You saw love withheld until apologies were earned. That became your normal. Now you're the adult repeating the same emotional patterns, shutting down when you're hurt, punishing with silence, saying "I'm fine" through clenched teeth because that's what strong people do, right? Wrong.

Strong people heal. Silent people hide. The limp isn't just in you; it's in the emotional atmosphere you create. Your children can inherit your mood before they ever hear your story. They may never know the details of what hurt you, but they'll grow up with the temperature of your pain.

If you're a parent, your limp teaches your children how to interpret hurt. If you're bitter, they'll learn to confuse forgiveness with weakness. They'll repeat your patterns, but they'll suffer your consequences. That's why this clinic isn't just about *you,* it's about your lineage. Because if you don't stop the limp, your children will learn to call dysfunction "family culture."

Ephesians 4:31–32 (NIV) puts it plainly: "Get rid of all bitterness, rage and anger, brawling and slander, along with every form of malice. Be kind and compassionate to one another, forgiving each other, just as in Christ God forgave you." Notice the word "get rid of." It's not passive. You can't pray bitterness away while protecting it. You must *avoid* it. You must confront it like a squatter in your soul. It's been living rent-free for years, and every time you justify your coldness with "I'm just guarding my heart," you're basically renewing its lease. Bitterness doesn't die by accident. It dies from exposure.

The Church Mask, Worshiping While Wounded

Bitterness doesn't just show up in family; it thrives in church culture too. We've built spiritual spaces where people can quote scripture fluently but can't apologize sincerely. You can pray in tongues but choke on "I'm sorry." You serve out of habit, not humility. You mentor others while secretly resenting the people you used to look up to. You hear sermons about love and think, *"If only they practiced what they preached."* You come to the altar, not to surrender, but to silently prove, *"See, I'm still showing up, even after what they did."* You've turned pain into performance. And while the congregation claps, your heart still limps out the door after every service.

Bitterness is like background noise in your faith. You may not always hear it, but it affects the way you interpret everything. A kind word feels suspicious. Correcting feels like criticism. Even God's discipline feels like rejection. Why? Because bitterness doesn't just affect how you see people, it affects how you see *God*.

When you're bitter, you stop believing God defends you. You start believing He's forgotten you. You confuse His patience with neglect. And you begin crafting an internal theology that protects your pain instead of your peace.

Bitterness will make you rewrite the gospel to fit your grudge. That's why this edition is called *The Gospel According to the Offended*. Because offense creates its own religion, one where you're always the victim, and everyone else is the problem. It's comfortable, it's righteous, and it's deadly.

The Cost Of Pretending

Let's strip away the pretense for a second. Pretending you're fine doesn't protect you, it paralyzes you. You can't heal from what you refuse to admit. You can't pray for transformation while defending the infection. Some of you are emotionally exhausted not because life is too hard, but because hiding has become your full-time job. You've curated a version of yourself that's strong, spiritual, and unbothered, but it's killing you quietly.

Bitterness eats joy like acid eats metal. It corrodes peace. It dulls empathy. It poisons your ability to celebrate others. It makes you allergic to vulnerability and addicted to control. And here's the hardest truth: you can't limp into new seasons expecting old pain to stay behind. You must deal with it, or it will deal with you.

Jacob learned that the hard way. He wrestled with God all night, and when the fight was over, God touched his hip, leaving him with a limp that marked him forever. But here's the difference: Jacob's limp came from encounter, not avoidance. It wasn't proof of pain; it was proof of presence. Your limp, however, came from holding on to things God told you to release. And every time you say, "I'm fine," you tighten your grip around what's been breaking you. But what if you let go? What if you stopped performing wellness and started pursuing wholeness? What if you gave God permission to touch what still hurts? What if your limp could become your testimony, not your identity?

Healing Is An Unlearning

To heal, you must unlearn how you've been surviving. You must unlearn how to walk in pretense. You must unlearn how to confuse  avoidance with forgiveness. You must unlearn how to see people through suspicion instead of compassion. You must unlearn how to use scripture to defend behavior Jesus died to deliver you from. You must unlearn the lie that being "fine" is spiritual. It's not. It's fatal.

The kingdom doesn't need your perfection; it needs your honesty.

The Body of Christ doesn't need more actors, it needs witnesses. People who can say, *"Yes, I was bitter, I was broken, but I stopped hiding and let God heal what pride was protecting."*

The world doesn't believe in our God because we don't show them our scars, only our filters. But every limp that's been touched by God carries power. It says, *"I was wounded, but I refused to let that wound define my worship."* You don't need to be fine. You need to be free. And freedom begins when you finally stop pretending.

🏷 FAITH PRESCRIPTION

Welcome back to your spiritual check-up. You've already admitted the symptoms and faced the x-ray. Now it's time for treatment. No painkillers here, just truth, repentance, and practice. Take with water, prayer, and a willingness to be uncomfortable.

1. Admit You're Still Bleeding

Confession isn't weakness; it is a release valve. The Kingdom's ER doesn't treat fake symptoms. Say it plainly: "God, I'm still angry. I still flinch when I see their name." Psalm 32 teaches that silence rots the bones; honesty revives the heart. Healing begins the moment you stop editing your pain for God's approval. He already saw the x-ray, you're just finally agreeing with the diagnosis.

Practical Step → Write one paragraph in your journal starting with, *"The part of me that still hurts is…"* Don't spiritualize it. Name it like you're handing it to a doctor.

2. Stop Rehearsing the Scene

Bitterness loves reruns. Every replay re-opens the wound. Replace rehearsal with release: every time the memory surfaces, speak life instead of replaying loss. Philippians 4:8 isn't a Pinterest quote, it's neurological warfare. Whatever is true, noble, right, pure, **think** on these things. The mind that keeps revisiting the pain becomes a shrine to it.

Practical Step → When the offense replays, whisper, "Lord, rewrite this memory with mercy." Then picture Him standing in that moment, calming your reaction.

3. Detach Without Dehumanizing

Yes, boundaries are biblical. But using distance as punishment is emotional witchcraft. Boundaries should protect peace, not feed pride. Forgiveness doesn't always rebuild relationships, but it does rebuild your oxygen supply. Ephesians 4:26 reminds: *"Do not let the sun go down while you are still angry."* Translation, don't let resentment get a full night's sleep in your spirit.

Practical Step → If you need distance, define it with prayer, not attitude. Tell God first, not group chat. Boundaries led by bitterness isolate; boundaries led by wisdom insulate.

4. Break Generational Contracts

If silence was the family's love language, rewrite it. Gather your children, your spouse, or even just your journal, and speak forgiveness into the air. Say their names, release the history. Your home becomes holy ground when confession echoes louder than complaint.

Scriptural Dose → Deuteronomy 30:19 *"I have set before your life and death, blessings and curses. Now choose life."* Choosing forgiveness is choosing life for generations you'll never meet.

Practical Step → Write two columns: "What I inherited" and "What I'm ending." Then pray over each "ending" with gratitude that the cycle stops with you.

5. Trade Pride for Presence

Pride says, "They'll notice I've changed." Presence says, "God, change me even if no one claps." You don't need an audience to heal; you need obedience to stay in the room while God operates. Bitterness is expelled through humility. James 4:10 *"Humble yourselves before the Lord, and He will lift you up."* Let Him lift, you stop performing.

Practical Step → Set aside 10 minutes of silence daily. No music, no multitasking. Just breathing and saying, "Search me, God." Stillness is the scalpel that pride avoids.

6. Replace Bitterness with Behavior

Forgiveness is not a feeling, it's a practice. You prove healing by acting opposite to the hurt. Send the text. Pray for the one who offended you (Luke 6:27-28). Speak blessing instead of proof. Even a whisper counts as progress: "Lord, bless them today." The tongue that blesses its enemy becomes a conduit of freedom.

Practical Step → Every week for 30 days, choose one act of undeserved kindness. Bitterness shrinks when generosity grows.

7. Rest Before You React

You can't detox while sprinting. Rest is not laziness, it's spiritual rehabilitation. When you pause, you give God time to translate your emotions before your mouth does. Isaiah 30:15 *"In quietness and trust is your strength."* Sometimes strength looks like a nap, a walk, or declining a debate.

Practical Step → Before responding to tension, inhale peace, exhale offense. Ask, "Am I replying from pain or from presence?"

8. Feed Faith, Not Frustration

Whatever you feed grows. Faith needs Word, worship, and community. Frustration feeds on gossip, comparison, and replaying memories. Switch diets. Proverbs 4:20-22 calls God's Word *"life to those who find it and health to their whole body."* That includes your emotional body.

Practical Step → Every time you want to vent, open Psalms instead. If David could process betrayal without losing belief, so can you.

9. Celebrate Tiny Recoveries

Healing rarely happens in dramatic revivals; it happens in daily choices. Every time you hold your tongue, that's recovery. Every time you pray instead of post, that's progress. Heaven throws a party over subtle obedience.

Practical Step → End each day by writing one line: *"Today I limped less."* By month's end, you'll have a record of resurrection steps.

10. Remember the Ultimate Physician

At the end of every treatment, the cure is not closure, it's Christ. Bitterness says, "They owe me." Grace says, "He paid for me." The cross is proof that healing always costs innocence, but freedom always wins. You don't have to defend yourself when Jesus already defended your destiny.

Prescription Summary → Take Truth daily, Forgiveness hourly, Grace as needed, and Pride only with food (humility). Refills unlimited. Expiration date: Never.

HOLY SPIRIT CONSULT

(The lights are dim. The room is quiet. The walls echo more honestly than words. You finally sit down on the edge of the hospital bed of your soul, still pretending you're fine. The chart in your hand feels heavy, not because it's full of information, but because it's full of denial. And then... He walks in.)

Holy Spirit: You've said, "I'm fine" so many times that even your tears don't believe you anymore. I've watched you say it through clenched jaws, rehearsed smiles, and long pauses between text replies. I've listened to the way your prayers shift from honest to edited, the way you tidy your emotions before bringing them to Me. But I never asked you to be fine. I asked you to be *real.*

You see, healing doesn't start with answers, it starts with honesty. You've been hiding strength because weakness makes you feel vulnerable, and vulnerability reminds you of the people who mishandled it before. But I am not them. I don't want to win. I expose myself to restore.

You think admitting the limp makes you look broken. I think admitting the limp makes you look like *mine.* I was there when the disappointment happened. I heard the words that still echo in your head. I saw the betrayal, the silence, the absence, the rejection. I also saw how you held it in your hands, promising Me you'd let it go… but secretly tucking it into your heart like a keepsake.

You didn't mean to keep it. You just didn't trust anyone to hold it without judgment. Every "I'm fine" you've whispered was a shield. Every "It's okay" was a disguise. And every time you walked away smiling, I walked beside you, feeling the pulse of pain you refused to name. You call it moving on. I call it limping in circles. Let's talk about that limp. It's subtle, isn't it? You only feel it when someone touches that old nerve, when you see their name, hear that tone, or notice someone doing what they did. You get cold, not because you're heartless, but because your body remembers what your mind keeps trying to bury. But here is the truth you keep dodging: you can't carry the cross and the grudge at the same time. One will always drop. And you've been dropping Me to carry them.

You: "But, Holy Spirit, they hurt me. They never said sorry. They got away with it."

Holy Spirit: And yet, I stayed. While they walked away, I stayed. While they lied, I listened. While you replayed the pain, I replayed My promise. You think forgiveness means pretending it didn't happen. It doesn't. It means trusting that *I saw it, and I'll handle it.*

You think forgiveness lets them off the hook. It doesn't. It unhooks *you.* You think forgiveness erases justice. It doesn't. It releases vengeance back into holy hands. I'm not asking you to forget; I'm asking you to stop letting your memory master your peace. You don't need another apology. You need release. You don't need them to validate your pain. I already did. Every wound they left, I marked with grace. Every scar they caused, I intend to turn into a testimony. I know you're tired. Pretending is exhausting. You've been "fine" for so long that you forgot what it feels like to breathe without bracing for impact. But today, right here, right now, you can exhale. Let Me hold what you've been hiding. Let Me press where it still hurts. Let

Me speak where silence has ruled. Because bitterness can't survive in the presence of truth.

You don't have to defend your limp anymore. You don't have to prove you're strong enough to walk it off. You just must let Me realign your steps. Jacob walked away from our wrestling limping, not because he lost, but because he finally surrendered control. You'll walk away too, different but delivered. I'll touch the same place they wounded, but this time, it won't be pain, it'll be power. So, here's your prescription: Stop hiding in "I'm fine." Start healing in "I'm here." I'm not waiting for the healed version of you to show up. I'm working with the broken one sitting right here. You're safe now. You can tell the truth. Because I already knew, and I never left.

🙏 GUIDED PRAYER

God, today I confess that 'I'm fine 'has been my favorite lie. I've hidden my bitterness behind busyness and called it strength. I've carried old wounds into new seasons and wondered why peace never stays. Create in me a clean heart, O God, and renew a right spirit within me (Psalm 51:10). Teach me to forgive without proof, love without leverage, and trust without saying wrongs. I surrender my limp for Your leading. I'm done pretending I'm okay. Heal me honestly, even if it means breaking my routine of pretending. Amen."

REFLECTION PAGE

1.   Who or what do you still mentally defend yourself against?

____

____

____

____

____

2. How has "I'm fine" shaped the way you parent, serve, or love?

____

____

____

____

1. What would honesty look like if you stopped editing your emotions before bringing them to God? Write a short letter to yourself beginning with, *"Dear me, it's okay to stop limping."*

____

____

____

____

____

____

____

🩹 **Journal Note:** Healing isn't about walking perfectly; it's about walking honestly. Every limp that leads you back to grace counts as progress.

Chapter 2:

Generational Grudges; The Family Tree Of Unforgiveness

⬤ SYMPTOM

Bitterness doesn't just appear one day like a bad mood; it's passed down like a family recipe. You may not even remember when you first tasted it; you just grew up surrounded by the flavor. In some homes, grudges are heirlooms. The family doesn't talk about emotions, they achieve them. Everyone learns early which topics are "off-limits," which relatives are "difficult," and which wounds are sacred enough to never be mentioned aloud. You think you're different until one day you open your mouth and your parent's tone falls out.

Generational grudges are emotional hand-me-downs. They fit just as poorly as the old clothes you swore, you'd never wear. You watched your mother hold it together while holding everything in. You watched your father use silence as armor. You thought it was normal to only show affection through sarcasm or to replace "I love you" with "Did you eat?" Those patterns became your emotional DNA.

The problem is, when pain isn't healed, it mutates. What your parent's called "strength" was often just survival. What they labeled "respect" was sometimes fear. And what they called "keeping the peace" was really code for "don't you dare bring that up again." Now you find yourself teaching your kids to be brave but not vulnerable, kind but never too honest, spiritual but emotionally unavailable. You're repeating cycles you never meant to inherit.

You see it in family reunions, that awkward tension between people who share a last name but not forgiveness. You see it in the sigh that escapes your chest every time your parent calls, or in the way you avoid certain relatives because it's easier than explaining the distance. You've learned to manage relationships like you manage pain, strategically and quietly. You convince yourself you've "set boundaries," but really, you've just built walls tall enough to keep everyone out, including healing.

Generational grudges are subtle because they hide behind culture, tradition, and pride. You hear phrases like "That's just how we are," or "Our family doesn't cry," or "We don't air dirty laundry." And while those sound like discipline, they're dysfunction. You're not protecting the family image; you're preserving the infection.

Maybe your childhood felt like a masterclass in pretending. You watched grown adults apologize through gifts, not words. You learned that anger was safer than sadness. You internalized that forgiveness was weakness, something only naive people did. But that's not faith, that's emotional inheritance disguised as personality. Bitterness is often disguised as "generational strength." You were taught to "never need anyone," and now you call your isolation "independence." You inherited control as a coping mechanism, thinking it was confidence. You don't trust people because your parents didn't, and now you spiritualize it by saying, "I just keep my circle small." But small circles can also be small prisons when built on fear.

The most dangerous part? You pass it down without meaning too. You tell yourself you're raising emotionally healthy kids, but your tone is proof that pain still lives in your bloodstream. You discipline out of frustration instead of guidance. You shut down when they ask real questions. You make them earn affection without realizing that you're teaching them how to perform for love, the same way you learned to perform for acceptance.

You can't lead your family to freedom while limping from inherited pain. That's how bitterness travels through bloodlines, not because God didn't break it, but because you kept feeding it through repetition. You repeat the arguments, the avoidance, the pride, and then pray for peace like you didn't just hand bitterness a microphone. Bitterness in families often hides under faith. You know the type, the family that prays together but doesn't speak to each other after "amen." The ones who worship side by side but haven't had an honest conversation in years. They'll pray for revival but can't handle reconciliation. You can quote 1 Corinthians 13 about love at the dinner table, but if forgiveness doesn't live there, love is just background noise.

And then there is the silent rivalry, the unspoken competition that lives between siblings or generations. Maybe you grew up feeling compared to someone who always seemed more successful, more spiritual, more stable. You promised yourself you'd never become them, but now your decisions orbit their approval. You're still proving something to people who aren't even paying attention anymore.

Bitterness becomes a family heirloom when no one has the courage to tell the truth. And the truth is, some of the people you've resented were also victims of what they didn't heal from. Your mother wasn't cold because she didn't love you, she was numb from carrying pain she didn't know how to name. Your father wasn't silent because you weren't worth words, he was ashamed of the man he didn't know how to become. They weren't withholding affection to punish you; they just didn't have a model for how to give it.

Understanding doesn't excuse pain, but it helps you stop recycling it. You can acknowledge what they did without continuing it. You can honor your parents without inheriting their patterns. You can love your family and still be honest about how they failed you. Because pretending they didn't is how the root stays alive.

Bitterness sneaks into your faith when you pray for generational blessings while secretly nurturing generational grudges. You quote

Deuteronomy about being the head and not the tail but skip over the parts about loving your neighbor as yourself, especially when that neighbor shares your DNA. And maybe, just maybe, you've been so busy trying to heal from your family that you haven't noticed how much of them live in you.

That is the catch: bitterness blinds you to your own reflection. You think you're protecting yourself from becoming them, but you're becoming what you won't forgive. Every time you replay the story, you reinforce the likeness. Every time you say, "I'll never be like them," you keep them alive in your spirit.

Generational grudges aren't broken by pretending your childhood didn't shape you. They're broken by dragging your family's emotional habits into the light, exposing the lies you were taught to call normal.

You can't heal what you protect out of loyalty. You can't break a curse you still defend as culture. And you can't expect your children to grow spiritually if they're growing up watching your grudges. The spiritual limp of your family may have been inherited, but the healing is optional, and it starts with you deciding that "I'm fine" ends here.

⚕ TEACHING

Bitterness loves legacy. It thrives in environments that confuse silence with peace and pride with identity. Families that never talk about their pain give it permission to build an altar. Every generation adds another brick until it looks like tradition. But the Bible doesn't call us to inherit emotional patterns; it calls us to break them.

In **Exodus 20:5-6 (NIV)**, God says, "I, the Lord your God, am a jealous God, punishing the children for the sin of the parents to the third and fourth generation... but showing love to a thousand generations of those who love me and keep my commandments." That's not a curse; it is a warning about consequences. God isn't saying He wants to punish families; He's saying pain left untreated multiplies faster than love left unpracticed. Every unhealed parent raises a child who thinks protection means distance. Every silent home raises an adult who makes mistakes quiet for safety.

 Generational grudges are like inherited debt, you didn't create it, but you're still paying interest. The interest looks like overreactions, control issues, fear of intimacy, sarcasm, and emotional exhaustion. You're spending energy trying not to become them, but every effort without healing just deepens the debt. To break this pattern, you must stop borrowing your family's definition of strength. Many of us were taught that strong people "don't cry," "don't talk about it," "don't depend on anyone." But Jesus wept, Jesus asked for help, Jesus depended on the Father, so maybe what your family called weakness was godliness.

When Jesus healed the man at the pool of Bethesda (John 5), He asked a strange question: *"Do you want to get well?"* That man had been paralyzed for 38 years. The answer should have been obvious, but Jesus knew something about human nature. We get comfortable with dysfunction. We learn to navigate pain so efficiently that healing feels inconvenient. Families do the same. They normalize bitterness until it feels holy. You can't uproot generational bitterness with half-truths. You must confront it spiritually and practically. Spiritually, by naming it, "Lord, my family struggles with anger, avoidance, unforgiveness." Practically, by doing the opposite, initiating hard conversations, expressing emotion, apologizing even when you weren't the only one wrong.

The spirit of bitterness is allergic to humility. It thrives in the atmosphere of pride and defensiveness. But humility breaks the cycle. The first person who apologizes becomes the first one free. That is why the devil fights reconciliation so hard, because one humble heart can dismantle decades of division. If you look at Joseph's story in Genesis, you'll see the perfect portrait of generational redemption. His brothers betrayed him, sold him, lied to him, and years later, when he had every right to retaliate, he wept instead. He told them in Genesis 50:20 (NIV), "You intended to harm me, but God intended it for good."

Joseph could have continued the family cycle of revenge, but he broke it with perspective. Forgiveness didn't erase his pain; it redefined it. God didn't remove the memory of betrayal, He repurposed it. That's the kind of healing you need: not selective amnesia, but holy perspective. Bitterness says, "They ruined me." Forgiveness says, "God redeemed it."

To break generational grudges, you must trade *inheritance for influence.* You don't owe your family silence to stay loyal; you owe them honesty to stay whole. You honor them by healing, not by hiding. And if you're a parent now, the healing must become intentional. Your children shouldn't inherit your triggers. They should inherit your truth. They should see you apologize. They should hear you pray for the same people you used to resent. They should learn that boundaries don't mean bitterness, they mean balance.

Every healed parent becomes a prophet of freedom for their lineage. You can literally rewrite emotional genetics by modeling grace instead of grudges. Your home becomes a living altar where the curse collapses and compassion begin. You're not responsible for how your parents handled pain, but you are responsible for how you handle theirs now. Bitterness dies when ownership begins. Stop waiting for them to change. You are the change.

If you want to see how quickly God redeems bloodlines, look at Ruth. She married into a broken family line, one cursed by famine and loss, but because she walked faithfully, her obedience brought restoration. Out of her lineage came David, and eventually, Jesus. That's what God does with surrendered generations. He turns bitterness into blessing when someone decides enough is enough. And maybe that someone is you. You might never get the apology you deserve.

You might never hear your parent say, "I was wrong." But God can still give you peace that apology couldn't. Forgiveness isn't waiting for them to change; it's deciding you won't stay chained.

There is a verse in **Romans 12:18 (NIV)** that says, "If it is possible, as far as it depends on you, live at peace with everyone." Notice that "as far as it depends on *you*." You can't control their healing, but you can end their hold. You can choose peace even if the people who hurt you never participate in it.

Generational grudges lose power when you stop playing emotional tug-of-war. Drop the rope. Walk away healed, not hardened. Healing your family history doesn't mean rewriting it. It means finally reading it out loud, acknowledging where the pain started, and deciding it stops with you. You are not cursed. You are called. And the moment you forgive what you've inherited, you change what your children will inherit after you.

FAITH PRESCRIPTION

So, you've finally realized it, bitterness didn't just knock on your door; it's been living in your family guest room for generations. Congratulations, you've just diagnosed the family secret no one wanted to name. Now, let's talk about treatment.

1. Identify the Family Symptoms, Not Just Yours

Before you can heal it, you've got to name it. Go back through your family stories, not to blame, but to understand. Was the home you grew up in full of yelling or silence? Did "I love you" sound like "Did you take the chicken out?" Did anyone ever apologize, or did people just wait for holidays to pretend nothing happened? Be honest: what emotions did your parents model? Anger, control, withdrawal, fear? What did they call "discipline" that was distance? This isn't dishonor, this is diagnosis. God isn't asking you to dishonor your bloodline; He's asking you to detox it.

Scripture Dose: *"The truth will set you free"* John 8:32 (NIV). The truth about your family will either sting or save you, but both are steps toward freedom.

Practical Step: Draw a "spiritual family tree." Instead of names, write patterns: "silence," "resentment," "perfectionism," "control," "avoidance." Then, circle what keeps reappearing, that's your generational infection site.

2. Stop Worshiping the Family Image

Some of us have turned "keeping the family name clean" into idolatry. You'd rather hide dysfunction than heal it because image control feels safer than truth-telling. But God doesn't bless cover-ups; He blesses confession. Jesus didn't die for your family's reputation; He died for your restoration. You're not being loyal when you lie to protect patterns. You're being loyal when you tell the truth that leads to healing.

 Scripture Dose: Proverbs 28:13, *"Whoever conceals their sins does not prosper, but the one who confesses and renounces them finds mercy."*

Practical Step: If your family avoids hard conversations, start with one. Not to blame, to build. Even if they don't respond, you've disrupted the silence that bitterness feeds on.

3. Repent for What You Repeated

Let's be real, you didn't just inherit pain; you've recycled it. You said you wouldn't yell like your father, but now your kids flinch when your tone changes. You swore you'd be open, but you've emotionally ghosted people the way your mom did. It's okay. Awareness is the first surgery; repentance is the suture. Repentance isn't guilt; it's redirection. It says, "I see it now, God, I refuse to carry it forward."

Scripture Dose: Ezekiel 18:20, *"The one who sins are the one who will die. The child will not share the guilt of the parent."* Translation: the curse doesn't continue unless you co-sign it.
Practical Step: Say out loud, "Lord, I break agreement with the bitterness I've inherited and repeated." Then, name one behavior you'll replace it with, apology, empathy, vulnerability, patience, silence that heals instead of silence that hides.

4. Relearn Love in Real Time

Unlearning generational habits means relearning holy habits. If your family's love language was guilt, learn grace. If it was performance, learn presence. If it was shouting, learn stillness. You cannot break bitterness with theory; you break it with practice. If your family never hugged, start hugging. If your family avoids emotion, start naming them. If your family spiritualized dysfunction, start praying *and* getting honest.

Scripture Dose: 1 Corinthians 13:4-7, Love is patient, kind, not proud, not self-seeking. That verse isn't poetic, it's prescriptive. Apply daily until symptoms subside.

Practical Step: Every week, choose one behavior your family avoided and model it differently. Example: "My mom avoided tears; this week I'll allow them." My dad never apologized; this week I'll say I'm sorry first." Small obedience rewires generations.

5. Bless What's Behind You

The end of bitterness is not silence, it's blessing. Forgiveness is not pretending nothing happened; it's releasing what happened from having power over you. When you bless your past, you stop letting it break your future. You say, "God, even that pain was a teacher." You stop rehearsing wounds and start rehearsing gratitude.

🧠 **Scripture Dose:** Romans 12:14, *"Bless those who persecute you; bless and do not curse."*

Practical Step: Write a short "benediction" over your family line. Example: "I bless my parents for doing the best they knew. I bless my grandparents for their endurance. I bless my lineage with peace, healing, and emotional honesty. The pain ends here." Read it aloud until it sounds believable.

6. Model the Breakthrough

Generational healing has receipts. Your children, your spouse, your siblings, they'll see it in how you respond when triggered. Every time you handle conflict differently, you're modeling deliverance. Every time you show grace instead of sarcasm, heaven updates the family record. You're not just healing yourself; you're editing the DNA of your family's emotional future.

🧠 **Scripture Dose:** Galatians 5:1 *"It is for freedom that Christ has set us free. Stand firm, then, and do not let yourselves be burdened again by a yoke of slavery.*

Practical Step: Journal a list titled *"Proof of Breakthrough."* Under it, record moments when you chose peace over pettiness, prayer over pride. Review it monthly, it's your evidence that the curse is collapsing.

7. Establish a New Family Normal

This is your new prescription: emotional honesty, spiritual humility, and verbal forgiveness. Stop making sarcasm your love language. Stop letting pride be your protector. Stop acting like confrontation is conflict. Your new family code is transparency, grace, and repentance on repeat. Teach your kids that love can be correct and still be kind. Teach your spouse that silence is not peace. Teach yourself that forgiveness doesn't mean reunion, it means release.

📖 **Scripture Dose:** Colossians 3:13 *"Bear with each other and forgive one another if any of you has a grievance. Forgive as the Lord forgave you."*

Practical Step: Choose a family phrase to replace "we don't talk about that. "Examples:
- "Let's talk this through."
- "That hurt me, but I want to understand."
- "We can fix this."

Make it your household mantra, the generational password that opens the door to healing.

	Prescription Summary	
Treatment	**Frequency**	**Purpose**
Honesty	Daily	Detoxes denial
Confession	As needed	Restores integrity
Apology	Immediately	Rebuilds trust
Grace	Hourly	Heals atmosphere
Rest	Weekly	Keeps you from burnout

📋 **Side Effects:** Unexpected joy, softer tone, lower blood pressure at family gatherings, and peace you didn't know existed.

Refill: Unlimited through prayer, therapy, community, and scripture.

🕊 HOLY SPIRIT CONSULT

I see you trying to be the strong once again, the one who keeps peace, who doesn't stir up old wounds, who pretends the past doesn't still echo in family gatherings. You've spent years acting like glue, holding everyone together, but what you don't realize is that you've been using pieces of yourself to do it. You inherited the role of "fixer" before you even knew what broken felt like. But child, hear Me clearly: I never asked you to carry the burden of everyone else's healing. I only asked you to let Me start with yours.

You've been carrying stories that were never yours to carry. Every sign you release has someone else's name hiding inside of it. I know the details of what they said, what they didn't say, and what they should've said years ago but never had the courage to. I saw the cold rooms you grew up in, where silence was survival and affection were rationed. I saw the strength you had to manufacture to make it look like everything was fine. You learned earlier that emotions were dangerous and honesty was expensive. But I have been waiting for the moment you'd stop performing and just let Me touch what you've been protecting.

You've been asking Me to heal your children, to bless your home, to make things right in your family, and I am. But healing begins with you, because healing is hereditary too. If bitterness can pass down through generations, so can breakthrough. The cycle ends when someone finally decides that silence is no longer sacred. And that someone… is you. Don't mistake this season as punishment; it's preparation. I'm not pulling you away from your family, I'm pulling you out of patterns. You've been rehearsing your family's survival tactics, but I'm teaching you new ones built on grace, vulnerability, and truth. The same mouth that used to defend pain will soon declare peace. The same heart that learned to protect itself will now learn to stay open.

You've believed the lie that healing means dishonor, that if you talk about what happened, you're betraying your family. But I say to you, you're not betraying them by breaking the pattern; you're blessing them. You are rewriting the emotional code of your bloodline. You are teaching your children that forgiveness is power, not weakness. You are showing heaven that what was once a curse can now become a covenant.

You've carried enough, beloved. You've apologized for emotions you didn't even cause. You've tiptoed around people's wounds to avoid awakening your own. But I am here, steady and patient, reminding you that it's safe to stop pretending. You can put the family secrets down now, I already know them, and I still chose you to break them.

You are not called to be the hero of your family's story; you are called to be the healed one. Let Me write the rest. I will take what was heavy and make it holy. I will turn every unspoken word into wisdom, every generational scar into strength. So, breathe. You don't have to perform anymore. You don't have to hold it all together. The world won't crumble if you cry. The legacy won't fall apart if you tell the truth. This is not the end of your family's story; this is the rewrite.

Let go of what you inherited in pain and make room for what you are building in peace. It ends with you, because I'm beginning again through you.

🙏 GUIDED PRAYER

Heavenly Father, I come to You carrying not just my own pain but generations of it. I realize now that some of the emotions I've been wrestling with didn't start with me, they started with those who came before me. The fear of speaking up, the habit of pretending, the pride that hides behind silence, they all have roots that reach deep into my family history. But today, I chose to stop watering those roots.

Lord, I confess that I've repeated things I said I'd never do. I've used the same tone I once hated hearing. I've shut down when I should have opened. I've been distant when I should have been gentle. Forgive me, God, for repeating what I was supposed to release. I can't heal what I keep hiding, and I don't want to live my life defending a pattern that keeps destroying peace.

You know my story better than I do. You saw what shaped me, the moments I wasn't seen, the words I never heard, the hugs I never received. And still, You've chosen to rewrite my story. You've called me to be a bridge between what was broken and what will be whole. So, I ask for courage, Lord, not just to forgive those who hurt me, but to forgive those who didn't know how to love me. Help me see my parents, my family, and even myself through Your eyes. Give me the grace to separate who they were from who You are. Let me stop confusing their silence with Your absence. I forgive them, not because it erases the pain, but because it removes the power that pain once had over me.

Break the generational habits that have traveled through my bloodline. Let my home sound different, feel different, and function differently. Let laughter replace tension. Let vulnerability replace pride. Let confession replace avoidance. God, if there are still words that need to be said, help me say them with love. If there are wounds that still need to be acknowledged, help me bring them into the light without shame. I trust You to do the surgery no therapist, no apology, and no apology post could ever fix.

Today, I stand as the interruption in my family's pattern. The silence ends with me. The grudges end with me. The emotional coldness ends with me. And in their place, I plant love, grace, and truth, all rooted in You.

Thank You, Father, for giving me the chance to heal what history tried to hand me. I am not a product of my pain; I reflect Your promise. What was broken in my family line will now become a testimony of restoration. In Jesus 'name, I declare: This ends with me, and peace begins with You. **Amen.**

REFLECTION PAGE

1. **Family Patterns Check:** Write down three emotional or behavioral patterns you noticed growing up. Which ones have you unconsciously repeated in your own relationships or parenting? *Example: "I learned to shut down during conflict," or "I confuse peace with silence."*

____

____

____

____

2. **Inherited vs. Chosen:** List the traits or habits that were passed down to you. Then, beside each one, write whether you choose to **continue** or **cancel** it. *Example: "Generational pride, cancel." "Hard work ethic, continue."*

____

____

____

3. **Letters That Heal:** Write a letter to your parents, grandparents, or any family member (living or gone) expressing what you wish they had said or done differently. You don't have to send it. This is between you and God, a step in releasing what they never knew how to carry.

____

____

____

4. **Rewriting the Script:** How will you model forgiveness differently in your home? Write one intentional action you can take this week to change your family culture. *Example: "Start weekly family prayer time," or "Apologize to my kids when I overreact."*

____

____

____

____

5. **Faith Declaration:** Finish this sentence in your journal: *"From this day forward, my family will be known for..."* (Speak it out loud, it's not just a goal, it's a prophecy.)

____

____

____

____

____

____

____

🩹 Final Note From The Faith Clinic:

Breaking generational patterns don't erase your family, it redeems them. Every healed response you give rewrites a spiritual DNA strand. You are not disrespecting your roots by growing beyond them. You're honoring the God who planted you to be the change.

📖 Faith Clinic Journal Page

Chapter 2: Generational Grudges
Date: _______________________________
Patient Name: ___________________________________

Emotional Status Check:
☐ Calm   ☐ Heavy   ☐ Reflective   ☐ Healing in Progress

💧 **Heart Notes:** What part of my family story still hurts when I think about it?

🌿 **Pattern to End:** One emotional habit or response I no longer want to pass down:

💬 **Words I Needed to Hear:** If someone in my family had said this, it might have changed everything:

💡 **New Family Legacy:** From this day forward, my home will be known for:

🙏 Mini Prayer

"God, teach me to bless where they broke me, and to model peace where pain used to live."
Signature: ___________________________________
Date: _____________________________________

Chapter 3:

Parents Aren't Perfect, But Neither Are You

⬤ SYMPTOM

You've spent years blaming your parents for what they didn't say, what they didn't teach, what they didn't become. And honestly, some of that blame feels justified. They weren't always kind. They weren't always patient. They didn't know how to talk about emotions or how to model forgiveness. Maybe they stayed when they should've left or left when they should've stayed. But here's the uncomfortable truth that no one likes to talk about: the same grace you think they don't deserve is the same grace you keep needing from God.

It's easy to analyze your parents through the lens of your pain, but it's hard to admit that you've inherited more of them than you'd like to believe. You hear their tone when you're frustrated. You feel their defensiveness when you're corrected. You find yourself reacting to people the same way they did, even though you swore you'd never. It's not that you're trying to become them, it's that unresolved pain will always reproduce itself until it's healed.

Bitterness toward parents often starts as disappointment. You grow up expecting them to be superheroes, wise, stable, emotionally present, but instead, you got flawed humans trying to survive their own battles. At first, you excused it. Then, you explained it. Eventually, you resented it. And somewhere in that resentment, you made a silent vow: *"I'll never be like them."* But life has a funny way of testing vows made in pain. Because the moment you become an adult, or worse, a parent, you realize that the job looks a lot easier than the passenger seat.

You've probably had that moment, the one where you're exhausted, stretched thin, and suddenly you hear yourself saying the same words you hated hearing growing up. Maybe it's "Because I said so." Maybe it's "You don't know how good you have it." Or maybe it's that sharp silence that communicates everything without saying a word. And it hits you; you've become what you judged. Not because you wanted to, but because you never truly forgave them.

Bitterness doesn't always show up as anger; sometimes it's coldness. You visit but never stay long. You talk but never go deep. You show up in the holidays but avoid eye contact when real conversations begin. You've learned to love with limits, a skill you picked up from watching them. You tell yourself you're setting healthy boundaries, but sometimes your "boundaries" are really walls built out of old expectations. You say things like, "I love them, but I just can't be around them too long." And while that may be necessary in some seasons, the danger comes when emotional distance becomes your only version of safety. Eventually, you start building the same kind of distance in other relationships too, with your spouse, your friends, even your children. Because bitterness toward a parent rarely stays contained; it becomes the filter through which you see every form of authority and love.

You want to honor your parents, but you don't know how to do that while still acknowledging the hurt. So, you swing between two extremes: suppression or explosion. Either you stuff it down and call it peace, or you finally speak up, but it comes out as anger, sarcasm, or passive-aggression. You can quote Ephesians 6:2 *"Honor your father and mother"* but deep down, you wonder if that command still applies when your parents were the ones who hurt you.

The truth is that honor doesn't mean ignoring their humanity. It means acknowledging it without allowing it to define yours. Your parents were imperfect, sometimes deeply so, but that doesn't mean you have to live as a product of their mistakes. Yet you can't walk in freedom while holding a grudge.

Let's talk about that grudge, the silent one you've been nurturing in the background of your life. You carry it every time you roll your eyes at their advice. You feed it every time you retell your childhood stories through the lens of what they didn't do. You reinforce it every time you say, "They'll never change." You've become fluent in bitterness while calling it maturity.

Maybe you've prayed for healing before. You've asked God to fix the relationship, but you secretly want Him to fix *them*, not *you*. You imagine reconciliation happening only after they apologize first. You want them to say, "I was wrong. I should've done better. You didn't deserve that." But what if they never do? What if they never say sorry? Would you still choose to heal, or will you stay emotionally stuck in the waiting room of their regret?

Bitterness is a strange addiction; it gives you the illusion of control. It makes you feel powerful because you're "the one who sees the truth," but it keeps you chained to the version of your parents who hurt you most. Every time you replay those moments, you keep reliving that powerless child instead of embracing the healed adult God is trying to grow you into. And here is the real kicker, one day, someone will look at you and see *their* source of pain. That's not an insult; it's perspective. Just as your parents were human, so are you. You'll get it wrong sometimes. You'll misunderstand. You'll speak harshly. You'll fail to show up the way someone needs you to. And when that happens, you'll understand just how fragile grace really is, and how desperately we all need it.

You're not a bad person for being hurt by your parents. You're human. But you'll stay bound if you let that hurt dictate your compassion. The truth is, God never told you to be your parents' judge. He told you to be His reflection. And reflections don't get to choose who they mirror. You can't claim to mirror Christ while holding contempt for the people who helped shape your story.

It's time to tell the truth: you can't become whole while holding your parent's hostage to a standard of perfection they were never equipped to meet. They were flawed, broken, and learning as they went, just like you. You're not the exception; you're the continuation. So yes, they messed up. They feel short. They wounded you, sometimes deeply. But now that you know better, are you doing better? Or are you repeating their silence with your own? Are you still shutting down during conflict? Are you still overcompensating by trying to be the "perfect parent," exhausting yourself in the process? Are you still blaming what happened to you for the way you treat others now?

Bitterness towards your parents might have started as defense, but it is now become delay. You've been waiting for them to change while God's been waiting for you to forgive. You've been praying for closure while Heaven's been offering healing. The only question left is: will you keep nursing the wound, or will you let God finally disinfect it? Because the truth is, you'll never be free from what you refuse to release, and you'll never become the parent, child, or believer you're called to be until you stop demanding perfection from people who were just trying to survive too.

⚕ TEACHING

Let's be honest, it's easier to talk about your parents 'failures than it is to face your own. It feels safer to keep pointing at their shortcomings than to admit that you've picked up some of the same habits. But healing requires humility, and humility starts with honesty.

Parents, by design, are supposed to reflect God's love, to protect, nurture, and guide. But when that reflection is cracked, the image gets distorted. You grew up trying to understand love through a broken mirror. And when love looks distorted long enough, you start believing that God loves the same way people did, inconsistently, conditionally, or only when you perform.

That is why bitterness toward your parents is so spiritually dangerous. It doesn't just poison your earthly relationships; it contaminates your theology. It causes you to approach God like a parent who's about to disappoint you. You brace yourself for abandonment. You wait for criticism. You anticipate rejection. You love Him cautiously; afraid He'll love you the same way your parents did, only when you behave.

The enemy loves that. Because if you project your pain onto God, you'll never experience His full peace. The devil doesn't need to destroy your faith, just distort it through disappointment. And one of his favorite filters is unresolved parental pain. So, how do you heal from that? You start by facing the truth: your parents weren't Villains, they were vessels. Imperfect, limited, sometimes emotionally unavailable, but still chosen by God to bring you into this world. Romans 8:28 doesn't say all things are good; it says all things *work together for good*. God didn't approve of their mistakes, but He knew how to weave redemption through them. You are not the product of their failure; you are the proof of God's faithfulness.

Forgiveness doesn't mean pretending they didn't hurt you. It means refusing to let their choices define your capacity to love. It means acknowledging the wound without giving it permanent residence in your identity. You can forgive someone and still maintain healthy distance. You can honor your parents without idolizing them. You can acknowledge their humanity without excusing their harm. But here is the hard truth: you cannot fully forgive your parents until you face your own parenting, even if you don't have children. You parent your friends, your siblings, your coworkers, and your inner child. Somewhere, you are modeling what you learned, consciously or not. The goal isn't to prove you're better; it's to become whole.

Forgiveness always begins with perspective. Imagine your parents not as the authority figures you remember, but as the scared, flawed, wounded people they probably were. Many of them didn't have healing resources. They weren't taught emotional intelligence, therapy, or even vulnerability. They were raised to survive, not to communicate. And survival isn't the same as strength; it's just the absence of death.

You can't change what they did, but you can choose what you do next. You can decide that the generational story changes with you. You can stop telling God how unfair it was and start asking Him how to grow from it. Bitterness says, "They owe me an apology."

Healing says, "God, teach me how to live without needing one." And maybe the apology you'll never get from them is the same apology someone else will one day need from you. That's how humility breaks the cycle. The moment you stop idolizing your pain, you start inviting purpose into it.

Ephesians 4:32 (NIV) says, *"Be kind and compassionate to one another, forgiving each other, just as in Christ God forgave you."* The standard for forgiveness isn't them; it's Him. God forgave you before you repented. He released you before you even understood your mistakes. That is the model. That is the grace you've been called to extend, not because they deserve it, but because you deserve peace.

When you forgive your parents, you free your heart to function the way it was designed, soft enough to feel, strong enough to love. You don't have to keep rehearsing your childhood. You don't have to keep proving your independence. You don't have to keep protecting yourself from ghosts of the past. You can live healed, not haunted.

And here is the beauty of it: once you stop expecting your parents to fill roles only God can, you'll start seeing them through compassion instead of critique. You'll realize that even in their mistakes, God was forming empathy in you. You'll understand that your pain wasn't wasted; it was training.

You may never have the perfect parent, but you can still have a perfect Father. And when you let that truth settle, bitterness loses its reason to stay.

⚕ FAITH PRESCRIPTION

You've spent years replaying what they should've done. Now it's time to start practicing what you can do differently. Healing from parental wounds isn't a one-time altar call; it is a lifetime posture of surrender, humility, and renewal. Here's your prescription plan, take daily, repeat indefinitely.

1. Acknowledge That They Were Human First

Before they were your parents, they were people with fears, flaws, and unfinished stories. You may have expected them to give you what they never received themselves. That's not an excuse, but it is perspective. When you start seeing them through grace instead of judgment, you'll realize that much of what they withheld wasn't cruelty, it was capacity. They couldn't give what they never had.

⚕ **Scripture Dose:** *"Father, forgive them, for they do not know what they are doing."* Luke 23:34 (NIV) That's not just about the people who crucified Jesus. It's about every parent who is parented out of ignorance, exhaustion, or fear. Forgiveness starts when you stop demanding repayment for something they didn't even know how to earn.

Practical Step: Write this sentence in your journal: My parents were imperfect, but they were not my enemy." Say it aloud until the truth feels lighter than the bitterness.

2. Release the Fantasy Version of Family

Part of what fuels bitterness is unrealistic expectation. You keep replaying what your childhood *should've been* like: hugs, words, safety and every replay make your reality feel more painful. But healing means mourning what didn't happen so you can make peace with what did. Let go of the imaginary parent you've been grieving. That version doesn't exist, and holding on to it only blinds you to the growth God is doing now.

℞ **Scripture Dose:** *"Forget the former things; do not dwell on the past. See, I am doing a new thing!"* **Isaiah 43:18–19 (NIV)**

Practical Step: Write a goodbye letter to the "ideal family" you imagined. Then, ask God to help you see the beauty that still came out of brokenness.

3. Repent for the Bitterness You've Nursed

You can't heal from what you secretly protect. Bitterness is like mold, it grows in dark, quiet places. You don't need to justify your feelings; you just need to bring them to the Light. Repentance isn't God shaming you for being hurt. It's Him freeing you from staying there.

℞ **Scripture Dose:** *"Create in me a clean heart, O God, and renew a right spirit within me."* **Psalm 51:10 (NIV)**

Practical Step: In prayer, list every emotion you've held toward your parents, anger, grief, disappointment, envy. Then, after naming each one, say, "I release this in exchange for peace." You can't receive what you refuse to release.

4. Apologize Without Expectation

You might not be the only one who needs to forgive, you may need to say, "I'm sorry" too. Not because you caused their pain, but because you've been withholding grace. Sometimes reconciliation starts with humility, not justice. Even if they don't respond, obedience is its own reward. You don't apologize for reaction; you apologize for reflection, because you see now what bitterness is costing you.

℞ **Scripture Dose:** *"If you are offering your gift at the altar and there remember that your brother or sister has something against you… first go and be reconciled to them."* **Matthew 5:23-24 (NIV)**

Practical Step: If it's safe and led by the Spirit, reach out. If not, write your apology in a letter and hand it to God. Either way, you release the debt.

5. Redefine Honor Through Healing

"Honor your father and mother" doesn't mean agree with everything they did. It means choosing respect without resentment. Honor isn't silence; it's stewardship. You can honor someone while acknowledging the hurt they caused. True honor is emotional maturity that refuses to retaliate. It's saying, "I will not speak about them with contempt, even if I still feel pain."

℞ **Scripture Dose:** *"Do not repay evil with evil or insult with insult. On the contrary, repay evil with blessing."* **1 Peter 3:9 (NIV)**

Practical Step: Each time you're tempted to criticize, bless them in prayer instead. You can't curse and heal with the same mouth.

6. Invite God Into the Memories

Healing doesn't erase the past, it redeems it. Invite God into those mental replays. When that memory surfaces, the argument, the abandonment, the unmet need, ask the Holy Spirit to show you where He was at that moment. He's not just rewriting your story; He's revealing that He never left it.

℞ **Scripture Dose:** *"The Lord is close to the brokenhearted and saves those who are crushed in spirit."* **Psalm 34:18 (NIV)**

Practical Step: In prayer, visualize that painful memory and imagine Jesus standing in the room. Let Him speak what you needed to hear then. Let Him rewrite the atmosphere with peace.

7. Practice Parenting from Healing, Not Hurt

If you're a parent, your children are watching your emotional habits. They're learning how to love, how to argue, and how to apologize by observing you. Don't make them inherit the same limp. Show them what healed looks like, not perfect, but present.

℞ **Scripture Dose:** *"Train up a child in the way he should go, and when he is old, he will not depart from it."* **Proverbs 22:6 (NIV)**

Practical Step: Tell your children one truth you wish your parents had told you. Give them the healing words you never received. It doesn't just repair them, it redeems you.

8. Let God Be the Parent You Needed

You may never get the nurturing you wanted from your earthly parents, but you can receive it from your Heavenly Father. He doesn't shame you for your scars; He calls them evidence that you've survived. He's patient with your emotions, gentle with your triggers, and present in every ache.

℞ **Scripture Dose:** *"As a father has compassion on his children, so the Lord has compassion on those who fear him."* **Psalm 103:13 (NIV)**

Practical Step: Sit in silence for five minutes today and pray, "Father, parent me through this." You'll feel His presence fill the space your parents never could.

Prescription Summary

Treatment	Dosage	Purpose
Grace	Daily	Softens your heart toward your parents

Forgiveness	Hourly	Keeps bitterness from returning
Perspective	Weekly	Reframes pain into purpose
Prayer	Constant	Reconnects you to peace
Gratitude	As needed	Shifts focus from lack to love

📋 **Side Effects:** Freedom, compassion, unexpected empathy, laughter returning to family gatherings, and the ability to talk about your past without reliving it.

🕊 HOLY SPIRIT CONSULT

You've been holding your parents 'names in your prayers and your pain at the same time, hoping I'd fix them while ignoring how tightly you're still holding onto the memory of what they did. I've watched your reply about conversations that ended years ago, trying to make sense of words that will never sound different. I've seen you pray for healing but clench your fists at the thought of forgiveness. But I need you to hear this, I'm not just trying to heal your past; I'm trying to make you whole in the present.

You keep asking Me to show you where your parents went wrong, but I'm trying to show you where grace can go right. You've spent so much time identifying their shortcomings that you've missed how I've been using them as mirrors, not to condemn you, but to correct your perspective. They weren't perfect, but neither were you. That truth isn't meant to shame you; it's meant to free you. Because perfection was never the goal, humility was.

I know they should have been different. I know you deserved gentler words, softer hands, and safer love. I saw the moments when you reached for affection and met silence. I felt disappointed when your effort went unnoticed. But I was there in those moments, too, not distant, not detached, present, grieving with you, holding what they didn't know how to hold.

I need you to understand something deeper: your healing doesn't depend on their apology. It depends on your surrender. You don't need their change to begin yours. I'm not asking you to forget; I'm asking you to forgive, because forgiveness is how you stop bleeding from wounds, they no longer touch.

Let Me reintroduce you to grace. Grace doesn't mean pretending they didn't fail. It means acknowledging that, even in their failure, I was faithful. You are not defined by the love you lack; you are defined by the love I've lavished on you since the moment you felt unseen. You are not the result of their mistakes; you are the result of My mercy. And I need you to release the fantasy version of them you've been holding hostage in your prayers, the version that apologizes perfectly, heals quickly, and meets all your expectations. That version isn't coming, but I am. I'm here to fill every space they left empty. I'm here to restore the voice you never heard and the touch you never felt. You don't have to chase their approval anymore; you already have Mine.

You've carried your childhood like a weight, but I'm turning it into a witness. What once made you hard will now make you holy. What once made you guarded will now make you gracious. You will parent differently, love differently, and forgive differently because you've finally seen what bitterness costs, and what peace restores.
So, let it go. Not because they deserve release, but because you deserve rest. You've been a child long enough, now become the healed one.

📖 DECLARATIONS JOURNAL

"Parents Aren't Perfect, But Neither Are You"

Instructions : Read these declarations out loud each morning this week. Then write your own reflection in the blank space after each one. Honesty is the only medicine that works here.

1. Declaration of Grace

I release my parents from the prison of perfection. They were never meant to be my gods, only my guides. I forgive them for what they could not give, and I thank God for what He gave me through them anyway.

Reflection: What has God taught me through my parents' imperfection?

2. Declaration of Humility

I am not flawless, I am forgiven. The same mercy I need daily is the same mercy I owe to others. I refuse to hold my parents to a standard I cannot meet myself.

Reflection: Where have I acted like the person I once resented?

3. Declaration of Healing

I will not rehearse old stories to justify new bitterness. The past cannot be undone, but it can be redeemed. I give God permission to rewrite my family history starting with me.

Reflection: What part of my family story needs God's redemption most?

4. Declaration of Release

I let go of the version of my parents I imagined. I accept the reality of who they are and who they aren't. And I still choose love, not because it is easy, but because freedom is too precious to lose.

Reflection: How can I love them now without losing myself again?

5. Declaration of Renewal

I am no longer raising children or relationships from my pain. I am parenting, loving, and living from my healing. The curse of comparison and resentment ends with me. Peace is my new inheritance, and grace is my new legacy.

Reflection: What legacy do I want my children or loved ones to inherit from me?

 Final Note: You're not rewriting your parents 'story; you're writing your own. Every word of forgiveness you speak is a seed planted for the next generation. Let them inherit peace, not proof of your pain.

🙏 GUIDED PRAYER

A Prayer for Releasing Parental Bitterness and Restoring Grace
Heavenly Father, I come to You today with a heart that's both heavy and hopeful. Heavy because I still feel the weight of what my parents couldn't give me, the love that fell short, the words that never came, the validation I waited years to hear. And hopeful, because I know You are the God who redeems every unfinished story.

Lord, I confess that I have held my parents to a standard they were never equipped to meet. I have spent years expecting healing to come through them when You've been offering it through Yourself. I've replayed their mistakes in my mind so many times that I forgot to notice the moments they tried, the small efforts that went unnoticed because I was still measuring them against perfection.

Forgive me, God, for letting bitterness sit where grace should have lived. You see the things I never said out loud, the disappointment, jealousy when I see others who had what I didn't, the ache that surfaces every time a memory reminds me of what could have been. I give those emotions to You now. Every word I wanted to hear, every hug that never came, every apology that never arrived, I lay them at Your feet. I'm tired of pretending I'm fine. I'm tired of holding grudges that only weigh me down. I need Your presence more than I need proof that they've changed.

Father, help me to see my parents through Your eyes, not as failures, but as fragile humans who did the best they could with what they knew. Let compassion replace criticism, and understanding replace resentment. If there are still conversations that need to happen, prepare my heart to speak truth with love and not accusation. If reconciliation is not possible, help me walk in peace anyway.

God, teach me to love from healing, not from habit. Where my parents modeled fear, let me model faith. Where they used silence, let me use gentleness. Where they withheld affection, let me give it freely. I refuse to pass on pain disguised as personality. I refuse to make my family carry the bitterness I didn't surrender.

Lord, heal the little version of me that's still waiting for a parent's approval. Remember me that I already have a Father who sees me, loves me, and calls me His own. Let that truth fill every empty space they left behind. Let it echo louder than any memory that once defined me. And God, if I've become the person who has hurt others while trying to protect myself, forgive me. If I've used my wounds as an excuse to wound others, wash me clean. Break the pattern, Lord, right here, right now, in me.

Today, I traded my anger for empathy, my expectations for surrender, and my hurt for Your healing. I release my parents, and in doing so, I release myself. I am free to honor them without idolizing them, to love them without losing myself, and to move forward without dragging the past.

Thank You, Father, for being the parent I needed all along, steady, safe, and patient with my process. You never left me. You never stopped teaching me how to love, even though people didn't know how. I choose peace. I choose perspective. I choose to forgive, not because they asked, but because You commanded, and because I finally understand that obedience brings freedom. In Jesus 'name, **Amen.**

REFLECTION PAGE

"Parents Aren't Perfect, But Neither Are You"

Date: _______________________________

Patient Name: _______________________________

🗭 **Heart Check:** What emotions still rise when I think about my parents or childhood?

____

____

____

____

🩺 **Spiritual X-Ray:** In what ways have I unknowingly repeated my parents 'patterns?

____

____

____

🗩 **Truth in Progress:** What's one thing I can do differently to show love where they didn't?

____

____

____

🌿 **Letting Go:** If I could say one thing to my parents without anger, what would it be?

____

____

____

🙏 **Faith Declaration:** "God, I forgive my parents for what they couldn't give, and I release myself from needing what they couldn't provide."

Signature: _______________________________

Date: _________________________________

Reflections

____

____

____

____

____

____

____

____

____

____

Chapter 4:
"They Owe Me an Apology" The Myth Of Closure

💧 SYMPTOM

You've been waiting for an apology that may never come, rehearsing the speech you'll give when they finally "get it," imagining the look on their face when they admit they were wrong, picturing yourself graciously forgiving them while silently thinking, *"Finally."* You've been keeping score in invisible ink, hoping God notices how long you've been the bigger person. But the truth is, you're not waiting for healing, you're waiting for vindication. And it's killing your peace one day at a time.

The myth of closure has convinced you that peace must be earned through someone else's remorse. You tell yourself that you can't move forward until they acknowledge what they did. You want them to confess, to say the right words, to understand the depth of how they hurt you. But what if they never do? What if they don't even remember the incident that has been replaying in your head for years? What if they truly believe *you* were the problem? What if they've moved on while you're still standing at the emotional crime scene? That is the twisted thing about offense, it freezes time.

Everyone else's life moves forward, but you stay trapped in that one conversation, that one betrayal, that one wound that never healed right. You call it "closure," but really, its control disguised as justice. You want to feel in charge of the ending, to make sure it's fair, tidy, and emotionally satisfying. But closure, the way you imagine it, doesn't exist. Not in this world.

You think if they just admit they were wrong, your heart will finally rest. But here is the hard truth: even if they apologized, it wouldn't erase the memory. It wouldn't undo the words they said or the ways they made you feel small. The pain wouldn't disappear just because they finally said, "I'm sorry." Because forgiveness isn't a transaction, it is a transformation. And until you let God do that work in your heart, no human apology will ever be enough.

Let's be honest, sometimes the person you're waiting for can't give you what you want. Maybe they're too prideful. Maybe they don't even see what they did as wrong. Or maybe they've already justified their behavior with their own narrative, and in their version of the story, *you* were the villain. It happens more often than we like to admit. Because people rarely remember the story the same way, they remember it in a way that makes them feel better about themselves. And so, you wait. Your reply. Your journal. You quote scriptures about forgiveness, but your tone still drips with resentment. You say, "I've forgiven them," but the conversation in your head proves otherwise. You're not at peace; you're on pause.

Maybe you even tried to make peace before, reached out, explained your feelings, extended grace, and they still didn't respond the way you hoped. So now you've sworn off trying. You call it "protecting your peace," but what you're really doing is hiding behind pride. You want reconciliation, but only if you can still control how it happens.

Bitterness feeds on the illusion of closure. It keeps whispering, *"If* 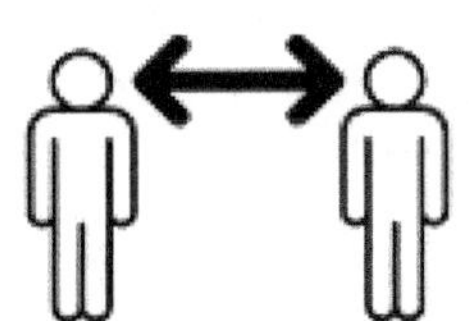 *they just owned up to what they did, you'd finally be free."* But freedom doesn't wait for their words, it begins with yours. The words you whisper to God when you finally admit, "I'm still holding this." The enemy loves to convince believers that unresolved hurt means unfinished healing. But sometimes God allows certain apologies to never come so He can teach you to rely on *Him* for closure. You see, if they apologized, you'd stop seeking God and start seeking validation. And God loves you too much to let someone else's remorse become your savior.

Let's talk about the emotional math of offense. You've probably kept a tally, how much you gave, how much they took, how unfair the exchange feels. You remind yourself of every detail to prove you're justified in your anger. But that ledger doesn't just record what they own it records what you've lost. Every time you check it, you relive the debt. Every time you replay it, you re-injure your own spirit. Closure, as the world defines it, says, *"I'll forgive when they admit it."* But the Kingdom says, *"Forgive because I forgave you."*

One requires apology. The other requires surrender. Here is the uncomfortable truth, sometimes people won't apologize because admitting guilt would cost them the identity they built around being "right." They'd rather keep their pride than own their pain. So, they rewrite the story to make themselves the hero. And you're left holding a version of the truth that only God seems to validate. That's where most people lose peace, in that in-between space where you know what happened, but the other person refuses to see it. You question your worth because of their blindness.

You confuse their silence with God's neglect. You start to wonder if forgiveness even matters when the offender gets to keep living like nothing happened. But that's where faith comes in, forgiveness is trusting that God sees what they refuse to admit. It's choosing to believe that divine justice is better than emotional revenge. It's surrendering the fantasy of "closure" and embracing the reality of freedom.

The hardest part is accepting that God might never give you the ending you wanted. There might never be a moment of dramatic reconciliation or heartfelt apology. You might never hear the words, "You were right." And you'll have to learn how to breathe through that. Because closure, in God's Kingdom, isn't something you receive, it's something you decide. Maybe closure isn't a conversation; maybe it is a conclusion, the one where you say, "I'm done carrying this." Maybe it's not about them realizing your value, but about you remembering it. Maybe it's not about them seeing their wrongs, but about you seeing your growth.

You keep asking God for justice, but sometimes His justice looks like peace while they stay the same. That's hard to swallow, isn't it? You wanted justice to mean public vindication, but sometimes God's justice is quiet, a healed heart, a peaceful mind, and a joy they can't take credit for. You'll know you've reached real closure when you can tell the story without bitterness in your voice, when you can talk about them without needing to prove how much they hurt you. You'll know you're free when you stop needing them to feel guilty for you to feel better. Because truthfully? They don't owe you an apology anymore. They owe God repentance. And you owe yourself peace.

⚕ TEACHING

The myth of closure has deceived many believers into thinking healing is dependent on another person's humility. But forgiveness is not a negotiation, it is a command. When Jesus said, *"Forgive, and you will be forgiven,"* He wasn't suggesting a fair exchange; He was describing a supernatural release. Closure, in the Kingdom, is not about completion of a conversation, it's about the cleansing of the heart.

In **Luke 23:34**, Jesus says from the cross, *"Father, forgive them, for they do not know what they are doing."* That's not just the picture of mercy; it is the blueprint of closure. Jesus didn't wait for His offenders to apologize. He didn't wait for them to realize their sin. He forgave them while they were still mocking Him. That's divine maturity, the ability to let go before anyone else is ready to say sorry. The world teaches you that closure is your right. God teaches you that closure is your release. One demands; the other surrenders. One drains; the other delivers.

The truth is, waiting for an apology is often just a way to delay accountability. If you can blame them, you don't have to heal. If you're waiting for them to make it right, you don't have to let God touch the wound. But God wants to deal with your pain even if the other person never changes. He doesn't need their cooperation to complete your healing.

Some believers confuse forgiveness with reconciliation. Forgiveness is spiritual; reconciliation is relational. Forgiveness happens between you and God. Reconciliation requires two humble hearts. Sometimes, it's not possible, not because God can't do it, but because the other person isn't ready. But your peace doesn't have to wait for their maturity.

Matthew 6:14-15 (NIV) says, *"If you forgive other people when they sin against you, your heavenly Father will also forgive you. But if you do not forgive others their sins, your Father will not forgive your sins."* That verse sounds heavy until you understand the freedom behind it, God isn't threatening you; He's protecting you. He knows that bitterness rots the heart from the inside out. Unforgiveness keeps you chained to an event that no longer exists. When you choose to forgive without apology, you're choosing to stop living in a time loop. You're saying, "I refuse to let a past wound control a present blessing." You're declaring that your peace is too expensive to rent out to resentment.

Closure is not found in their confession; it's found in your release. It's not about fixing what happened; it's about surrendering what's left. Some of you are still praying for God to "make them see what they did," but what if He's trying to make *you* see how much power you've given them over your emotions? You've let their silence dictate your joy, their pride dictates your perspective, and their absence dictates your identity. But you don't need their understanding to validate your healing. You only need God's.

There's a story in 1 Samuel 25 about a woman named Abigail. Her husband, Nabal, insulted David, provoking David to vengeance. Abigail intercepted David with wisdom and humility, saying, *"Please pay no attention to that wicked man Nabal. He is just like his name, his name means Fool, and folly goes with him."* (v.25). She took responsibility for something she didn't even do to prevent greater harm. That's what closure sometimes looks like, being wise enough to step between offense and overreaction. Abigail didn't wait for her husband to apologize; she moved with discernment. And in the end, God handled the justice.

The same God who avenged David will handle yours. You don't need to script the apology. You just need to surrender the outcome. If you're honest, what you really want isn't just an apology, it's acknowledgment. You want someone to say, "You were right. You didn't deserve that. You mattered." But what if you let God be the one to tell you that? He already has. Every time you come to Him in prayer, He whispers, *"I saw it. I was there. And I'm still here."*

You don't need them to validate your pain for it to be real. You just need to stop renting your healing space to their absence. Here is hard truth: closure doesn't always look like reconciliation. Sometimes closure looks like peace that no one else understands. Sometimes it looks like you are walking away with your dignity intact and your hands empty. Sometimes it looks like you finally accept that you may never hear the apology and realize you're okay with that.

God's version of closure often feels one-sided because it's built on trust, not fairness. When Joseph forgave his brothers, they didn't apologize at first. When Jesus forgave Peter, Peter was still drowning in guilt. Forgiveness always starts with the one who has the courage to go first.

Forgiving without an apology isn't a weakness, it's worship. It says, "God, I trust You more than I trust my feelings. I trust Your justice more than I trust my own." And when you do that, you create space for God to restore what bitterness destroyed.

Romans 12:19 (NIV) says, *"Do not take revenge, my dear friends, but leave room for God's wrath, for it is written: 'It is mine to avenge; I will repay, 'says the Lord. "* In other words, let God handle the courtroom while you focus on your recovery. Because here's the irony, when you finally stop waiting for their apology, you realize that peace was never about what they owed you; it was about what you were holding onto. You've been standing at a closed door, begging for them to open it, not realizing God already built you a new house.

Real closure isn't a conversation, it is conviction. It's when you finally believe that God's validation is enough. You may never get to hear "I'm sorry." But one day, you'll tell your story and realize you're not angry anymore. You'll stop needing them to see what they did because you'll finally see what God did through it. And that, that's closure.

⚕ **FAITH PRESCRIPTION**

When You're Waiting on Words That May Never Come
So, you're waiting for the apology, huh? The one that's going to make everything click, the conversation that will finally put a period where there's been a comma for years. You've rehearsed it in your mind: they'll say, "I was wrong," you'll say, "I forgive you," and angels will start humming in the background. Cute, but not how it works. The truth is, you don't need closure from them when you've got confirmation from God. Healing doesn't start with "I'm sorry"; it starts with "I surrender." Here's your treatment plan, spiritually prescribed, divinely backed, emotionally effective:

1. Diagnose the Real Problem, Control Disguised as Justice

You've been telling everyone you're "waiting for closure," but let's call it what it is: control. You don't just want them to apologize to you, you want them to apologize *the right way,* with the right tone, at the right time, fully understanding how deeply they hurt you. But that's not closure; that's choreography.

℞ **Scripture Dose:** *"Vengeance is mine, I will repay," says the Lord.* Romans 12 :19 (NIV)

Practical Step: Write down what you wish they'd say every word. Then look at it, take a deep breath, and tell God, "This is Yours now." You're not giving up justice; you're giving up the illusion of control.

2. Stop Worshiping the Word 'Sorry'

Some of you treat "sorry" like salvation. You believe that if you could just hear those two syllables, your soul would exhale. But here is the thing, an apology doesn't resurrect trust. It doesn't rebuild time. And sometimes it's not even sincere.

℞ **Scripture Dose:** *"People look at the outward appearance, but the Lord looks at the heart."* **1 Samuel 16:7 (NIV)**

Practical Step: Start measuring healing by obedience, not apologies. Ask yourself, "Have I obeyed God in forgiveness?" not "Have they confessed yet?" Obedience always produces more peace than validation ever could.

3. Forgive Before They Ask

Jesus forgave before anyone even thought about repenting. While they mocked Him, He said, *"Father, forgive them."* That's what Kingdom maturity looks like, releasing people while they're still wrong.

℞ **Scripture Dose:** *"Be kind and compassionate to one another, forgiving each other, just as in Christ God forgave you."* **Ephesians**

4:32 (NIV)

Practical Step: Pray this prayer: "God, I release them before they even realize what they did. I forgive them while they're still blind, because I refuse to stay bound." Do it daily until your spirit believes it more than your emotions resist it.

4. Accept That Closure Is a Myth, Peace Is Not

Closure is something the world invented to make pain sound polite. But God never promised closure. He promised *peace that surpasses understanding* (**Philippians 4:7**). That means even if you never understand, you can still rest.

℞ **Scripture Dose:** *"You will keep in perfect peace those whose minds are steadfast, because they trust in you."* Isaiah 26:3 (NIV)

Practical Step: Replace the word "closure" in your prayers with "peace." Stop saying, "God, give me closure." Start saying, "God, give me peace that doesn't need answers."

5. Remember: They May Never Get It, And That's Okay

The hardest truth to swallow is this, some people will never understand how much they hurt you. They'll go to their grave believing they were right. But your peace doesn't depend on their awareness; it depends on your will.

℞ **Scripture Dose:** *"As far as it depends on you, live at peace with everyone."* **Romans 12:18 (NIV)**

Practical Step: Release the expectation of "mutual understanding." You don't need them to agree with your version of events; you need God to rewrite how it affects your heart.

6. Let God Handle the Justice Department

You are not the Director of Divine Affairs. You don't have to supervise karma, manage outcomes, or monitor whether they're "getting what they deserve." God saw it. God remembers. God will handle it.

℞ **Scripture Dose:** *"He will make your righteousness shine like the dawn, your vindication like the noonday sun."* **Psalm 37:6 (NIV)**

Practical Step: Every time you're tempted to replay the offense, say out loud: "That's not my courtroom anymore." And mean it. God's gavel always hits harder and fairer than yours ever could.

7. Replace the Closure You Want with the Confidence You Need

Stop craving emotional payback and start cultivating peace that can't be shaken. Closure is overrated; confidence in God is not. You don't need the ending you planned to live the future He promised.

℞ **Scripture Dose:** *"The Lord will fight for you; you need only to be still."* **Exodus 14:14 (NIV)**

Practical Step: Each morning, write this declaration somewhere visible: "I don't need closure when I have Christ." Repeat it until it's not just true on paper, it's true in your heart.

8. Redirect the Energy of Waiting

You've spent months, maybe years, waiting for them to change. Imagine if you redirected that same energy into your growth, your prayer life, your purpose. Waiting for drains. Working on yourself heals.

℞ **Scripture Dose:** *"Let us throw off everything that hinders and the sin that so easily entangles."* Hebrews 12:1 (NIV)

Practical Step: For every minute you want to vent about what they did, spend that minute declaring what God is doing. Offense will lose its oxygen when you start breathing gratitude again.

9. Practice Silent Forgiveness

Sometimes the loudest forgiveness is the kind no one ever hears. You don't need to announce your growth to prove it's real. You don't have to post about your boundaries for them to be valid. Let your peace speak louder than your pain.

℞ **Scripture Dose:** *"Do not let your left hand know what your right hand is doing."* **Matthew 6:3 (NIV)**

Practical Step: Choose one person who hurt you. Instead of texting or confronting, simply pray, "God, bless them." Do it again tomorrow. Forgiveness matures in silence.

10. Choose Peace Over Proof

Closure demands evidence. Forgiveness demands faith. You can spend your life trying to prove how wrong they were, or you can spend it showing how free you are.

℞ **Scripture Dose:** *"Let the peace of Christ rule in your hearts."* Colossians 3:15 (NIV)

Practical Step: Write this in your journal: "Their apology isn't my proof. My peace is." Because when you stop needing closure from people, you'll finally start experiencing completeness in God.

Prescription Summary

Treatment	Dosage	Purpose
Forgiveness	Daily	Loosens bitterness at the root
Trust	Constant	Transfers justice from your hands to God's
Perspective	Morning + Night	Remember your heart, it's not about fairness
Silence	As Needed	Keeps peace sacred
Gratitude	Hourly	Redirects energy from pain to purpose

📃 **Side Effects:** Unexpected calm, increased clarity, the ability to tell your story without resentment, and peace that makes people wonder what changed.

🕊 HOLY SPIRIT CONSULT

You keep asking Me to make them see what they did. You want them to understand, to feel it, to own it. You say you're ready to forgive, but what you really mean is you're ready, *if* they apologize first. I hear the ache behind your prayers, the quiet exhaustion of trying to get someone else's confession to heal your wound. But child, that's not how healing works.

You think closure will make you whole, but closure is just another word for control. You want to close the chapter your way, with clarity, justice, and validation. But I didn't call you to close. I called you to completion, and that's something I do, not them.

I know what they said. I saw the betrayal. I felt the sting when they turned your honesty into ammunition. I was there when your words were twisted, your intentions misunderstood, and your character questioned. I didn't miss a single detail. But I need you to trust Me with what you can't fix.

You've built an emotional courtroom, replaying the evidence in your mind. You've called witnesses, revisited memories, and delivered verdicts that keep you imprisoned while they walk free. You don't even realize you're the one doing time. Let Me take the gavel. You were never meant to be both the wounded and the judge.

I know how much you crave their "I'm sorry." I know it feels unfair that they get to live unbothered while you're left cleaning up the emotional wreckage. But I never promised fairness. I promised freedom. And freedom doesn't wait for fairness to happen. You keep asking for closure, but what you really need is to surrender. Stop looking for resolution in their words; find it in Mine. You're waiting for them to acknowledge your worth, but I already did when I called you Mine. You're waiting for them to admit what they broke, but I've already begun to rebuild you. They can't give you peace, they're the reason you came looking for it.

It's time to let go of the need to be right and embrace the call to be healed. The apology you're waiting for may never come, but the healing I've been offering is already here. You can have peace without proof. You can have joy without justice. You can walk away whole even if the story never feels complete.

Stop holding your heart hostage to the hope of their change. I am closure enough for every wound they cause. When you forgive without an apology, you don't lose power to reclaim it. Because in that moment, you stop being the victim of their silence and start being the vessel of My Spirit. They don't owe you an apology anymore. I already paid for it on the cross.

📖 DECLARATIONS JOURNAL

"They Owe Me an Apology, The Myth of Closure"
Instructions : Read these declarations slowly. Say them out loud until your heart catches up with your mouth. Then write your reflection in the space below each one, not to explain, but to release.

✚ 1. Declaration of Release
I no longer need an apology to move forward. My peace is not held hostage by their words. I choose to let go, not because they were right, but because I refuse to live wronged.

Reflection: Who have I been waiting on to "make it right"?

____

____

____

____

💬 2. Declaration of Trust

I trust God to handle what I can't. He saw what they did. He heard what I couldn't say. Justice is His job. Healing is mine.

Reflection: What do I still need to surrender to God's justice instead of my control?

____

____

____

____

🌿 3. Declaration of Peace

Peace is my inheritance, not a prize I have to earn. I stop chasing closure and start walking calmly. Even without answers, I am complete in Christ.

Reflection: What does peace look like for me, practically, daily, honestly?

____

____

____

____

💧 4. Declaration of Strength

I don't need them to understand my pain to validate my growth. My strength is not found in their remorse; it's found in my decision to rise.

Reflection: How has my pain made me stronger, wiser, or softer toward others?

____

____

____

____

◈ 5. Declaration of Identity

I am not what happened to me. I am who God healed me to be. Their silence no longer defines me. His Word does.

Reflection: What truth from God's Word will I stand on when the hurt resurfaces?

____

____

Final Note: Closure isn't a destination, it's a decision. You decide that today's peace is more valuable than yesterday's pain. And when you do, that's not weakness. That's victory in progress.

🙏 GUIDED PRAYER

A Prayer for Release, Peace, and Trusting God with Justice
Father, you see my heart better than anyone else. You know the words I've been waiting to hear, the "I'm sorry," the "you were right," the "I finally understand." You know how long I've carried the weight of silence, trying to make peace with the ache of

unfinished conversations. And Lord, if I'm honest, I'm tired. I'm tired of waiting for someone else's repentance to make me feel whole again.

God, I confess that I've been holding on to the idea that closure would heal me. I thought if they apologized, the wound would close and the pain would stop. But I see now that I've been mistaking their words for Your work. I've been waiting for a person to do what only Your presence can.

Lord, help me release my need to be right, to be understood, and to be vindicated. You saw everything they did, the things they said, the moments they ignored, the ways they misunderstood me, and still, You call me to forgive. It feels unfair, but I'm learning that forgiveness isn't about fairness; it's about freedom.

Today, I chose freedom. I release them into Your hands, not because they earned it, but because I can't afford to carry them anymore. Every replay in my head, every argument I rehearse, every version of "closure" I've been imagining, I give it all to You.

Father, if I'm honest, part of me wants them to feel what I felt. But then I remember that Your justice doesn't look like revenge; it looks like redemption. So, I let go of revenge. I trust You with the outcome. I trust that You're not ignoring what happened, You're just healing it differently than I expected.

Heal my pride, Lord. Heal my obsession with being validated by those who hurt me. Remind me that Your "Well done" is louder than their silence. Remind me that my value isn't up for negotiation based on who apologizes or who doesn't.

Teach me how to find peace without proof. Let Your voice drown out every echo of their absence. Let Your love replace every word they never said. Fill the empty space with Your presence, the kind that *doesn't need explanations to bring comfort. And Lord, help me stop rehearsing their apology in my mind and start rehearsing Your promises instead. I don't need closure when I have Christ. I don't need their understanding when I have Your unfailing love. I don't need them to see my side when You've already seen my heart. Give me courage to walk away from the need for resolution and into the reality of peace. Let my forgiveness become my final act of closure. Today, I declare that I am not waiting anymore. I'm walking free. In Jesus 'name, **Amen.***

REFLECTION PAGE

"They Owe Me an Apology. The Myth of Closure"
Date: _______________________________________
Patient Name: _______________________________

⚬ **Heart Check:** Who am I still waiting to apologize before I feel free?

____

____

⚬ **Spiritual Diagnosis:** What emotion do I feel when I think about their silence, anger, sadness, pride, or disappointment?

____

____

____

⚬ **Treatment Plan:** What would peace look like for me if the apology never came?

____

____

____

____

____

⬤ **Faith Declaration:** God, I choose peace over proof, surrender over control, and freedom over waiting for what may never be said."

🫧 **Discharge Note:** Closure is not a conversation; it is conviction. I decided today that their silence will no longer interrupt my healing.
Signature: _______________________________
Date: _______________________________

📖 DECLARATIONS JOURNAL

"They Owe Me an Apology, The Myth of Closure"
Instructions : Read each declaration aloud. Let it confront you, comfort you, and challenge the version of you that's still waiting for someone else's repentance to validate your peace. Then journal your personal response in the space below each one.

💬 1. Declaration of Freedom

I am not waiting anymore. The apology that never came will no longer control my emotions or delay my growth. I don't need closure when I have Christ, and I don't need an explanation when I already have peace. What they left unfinished, God is completing in me.

Reflection: What do I need to release to move forward with peace?

⬥ 2. Declaration of Justice

I trust God to handle what I cannot. His justice is not delayed; it's divine. Every injustice that went unspoken, every moment that went unseen. He saw it all. I don't have to play the judge when the real Judge is already ruling in my favor.

Reflection: Where do I still feel the need to prove I was right?

⬥ 3. Declaration of Surrender

I no longer chase closure from people who never intended to give it. I will stop replaying what should have been said and start remembering what God already spoke over me. I trust His timing, His way, and His version of justice. I will not rewrite the story to make it fair, I'll let Him redeem it to make it fruitful.

Reflection: How has God already brought good from what once felt unfair?

⚕ 4. Declaration of Healing

Their silence will not speak louder than God's healing. I will not define my worth by who admits they were wrong. I am not the victim of their choices. I am the testimony of God's mercy. I choose healing over holding on, peace over proof, and joy over justice.

Reflection: How can I tell my story now without bitterness in my tone?

◈ 5. Declaration of Identity

I am whole even without closure. I am validated by God, not by people. I don't need the past to make sense when my purpose still makes progress. Every unanswered apology is now an altar, a place where I lay down pride and pick up peace.

Reflection: What does wholeness look like for me right now, in this season?

____

____

____

____

Final Thought: You don't need their words to heal when God's Word already said, *"You are free."* Closure is not about what ends, it's about what you decide won't hold you anymore.

Reflections

____

____

____

____

____

____

____

____

____

____

Chapter 5:

The Silent Treatment Isn't Spiritual Warfare

SYMPTOM: *Using distance and coldness as punishment disguised as "boundaries."*

You don't slam doors anymore. You don't yell or argue. You've matured, or at least that's what you tell yourself. Instead, you've learned the fine art of going quiet. You've convinced yourself that silence is strength, that ignoring someone is the holy version of "guarding your peace." You call it "protecting your boundaries," but really, it is a controlled freeze, an emotional shutdown disguised as spiritual maturity.

You've turned the silent treatment into your superpower. When you're hurt, you withdraw. When you're disappointed, you disappear. When someone confronts you, you retreat to that spiritual high ground called "I just need time to pray." And while prayer is powerful, sometimes what you call prayer is really avoidance in worship clothes.

Let's be honest, silence can feel safe when words have been weapons in your past. You've been misunderstood before, accused before, dismissed before. So now, you guard your voice like it's a vault. But here's the problem: in trying to protect yourself from pain, you've also locked yourself away from healing. You don't realize it, but your silence speaks volumes. It communicates rejection, pride, and punishment, even if you tell yourself you're "just processing."

You've mastered what I call the *holy ghosting technique*, when you vanish emotionally or physically while pretending it's God's will. You convince yourself that pulling away is obedience, but deep down, you know its protection mixed with pride. It's easier to call distance "discernment" than to admit you're angry. It's easier to say, "I'm setting boundaries" than to confess, "I'm being petty."

Now, let's not confuse boundaries with bitterness. Healthy boundaries protect peace; emotional walls protect pain. There's a difference. Boundaries say, "I love you, but I need space to heal." Walls say, "I'm done with you until you realize how wrong you were." One invites accountability. The other enforces punishment.

And punishment is exactly what the silent treatment is. Its control is dressed in maturity. You get to decide who gets access, who gets ignored, and for how long. You create a system where people have to "earn" your conversation again, like they're on probation for hurting your feelings. You may not raise your voice, but you still want them to feel the sting of your absence. You don't need to throw words when you can throw silence.

Let's call it what it really is: manipulation. Silent treatment says, "I'm going to withhold connection until you meet my unspoken expectations." It's emotional warfare, not spiritual warfare. You may be quoting scriptures during your quiet streak, but heaven isn't applauding your discipline; it's grieving your disconnection.

You've mistaken withdrawal for wisdom. But silence doesn't always mean healing; sometimes it means hiding. God can't restore what you won't talk about. He can't reconcile relationships if you've already decided they're unworthy of your voice.

You tell yourself that you're "just matching energy," but matching dysfunction is not deliverance, it's duplication. The same pride that hurts you is the pride you're now using to defend yourself. Bitterness never shows up as rage in mature people, it shows up as distance.

You stop fighting for peace and start protecting your pain. You tell yourself you're unbothered, but you're unsettled. And let's talk about how spiritually we make this look. You quote verses about "guarding your heart" (Proverbs 4:23), but you're really guarding your grudge. You use "be still and know" (Psalm 46:10) as an excuse to give people the cold shoulder. You spiritualize your withdrawal to make yourself feel righteous, as if silence automatically equals holiness. But being unresponsive isn't always spiritual, sometimes it's selfish.

Don't get me wrong, there are moments when God calls for quiet. There's power in stillness, strength in self-control, and wisdom in restraint. But there's a big difference between godly stillness and passive-aggressive silence. Stillness brings peace.

The silent treatment brings punishment. One invites healing; the other delays it. Maybe you've been so conditioned to equate silence with strength because in your past, speaking up caused more harm than good. Maybe your words were used against you, so now silence feels safe. But when safety becomes your strategy, you start mistaking isolation for identity. And that's exactly what the enemy wants, for you to hide behind self-righteous distance and call it discernment.

The longer you stay silent, the louder bitterness grows. Silence gives resentment space to multiply. You start imagining narratives, assuming motives, and writing scripts for conversations that never even happened. You convince yourself that your silence is "keeping the peace," but really, it's keeping you in pieces.

And the saddest part? People who once loved you start walking on eggshells around your silence. They can feel the chill in the room, even if you never say a word. The relationship becomes a guessing game, and everyone loses.

The silent treatment doesn't fix broken trust. It just freezes it. The longer you withhold communication, the more distance you create, not just emotionally, but spiritually. You start missing out on the lessons God was trying to teach through that relationship because you've muted not just them, but Him.

Here is the truth you've been avoiding: the same silence you're using to punish others is the same silence that's keeping you from peace. It feels powerful, but it's poisonous. It numbs the wound temporarily but never cleans it. You don't get healed by withholding; you get healed by honesty. You can't use silence to punish and expect it to produce peace. You can't use withdrawal to prove a point and expect it to build relationship. And you can't call yourself emotionally healthy while weaponizing distance. Your silence doesn't make you strong; it makes you stuck.

⚕ TEACHING

Relearning emotional honesty without guilt or manipulation.
Let's be real, we've all used silence to make a statement. We've all pulled away from someone to "teach them a lesson," hoping they'd notice the change and crawl back with remorse. But here's what God wants you to learn: true maturity isn't in mastering the art of withdrawal, it's in learning how to communicate with grace.

Bitterness thrives where communication dies. When we shut down instead of speaking up, resentment festers in the dark. That is why Ephesians 4:26-27 (NIV) says, *"In your anger do not sin. Do not let the sun go down while you are still angry, and do not give the devil a foothold."* Notice that anger isn't the sin; silence is when it becomes a breeding ground for bitterness.

God isn't impressed by how long you can stay quiet. He is moved by how quickly you can choose reconciliation. Real boundaries are built with honesty, not avoidance. Silence may feel spiritual, but Scripture calls us to confession, forgiveness, and restoration, all of which require communication.

Emotional honesty is not the same as emotional exposure. You don't have to overshare or vent to every person who hurt you. But you do have to stop pretending that silence equals resolution. Maturity doesn't mean never feeling, it means feeling and still choosing to handle it God's way. So, what does emotional honesty look like? It looks like being able to say, "That hurt me," without needing to humiliate someone. It means being able to express disappointment without detachment. It means learning to confront conflict with clarity, not coldness.

Jesus modeled emotional honesty perfectly. In Matthew 26, when He felt anguish before the cross, He didn't isolate Himself in silence, He brought His feelings before the Father and His disciples. He said, *"My soul is overwhelmed with sorrow to the point of death."* (v.38). That's emotional honesty. He didn't fake peace. He brought His pain into prayer.

You've been trying to use silence to heal, but silence doesn't heal, it hardens. Healing happens through vulnerability. When you finally admit, "That situation wounded me," you make space for the Holy Spirit to enter what you've been protecting. But if you hide behind pride, God can't fix what you refuse to expose.

Colossians 3:13 (NIV) says, *"Bear with each other and forgive one another if any of you has a grievance against someone."* That verse doesn't say, "Avoid them and call it peace." It says *bear with them,* which means endure, communicate, forgive. Healing relationships take conversation, not cold shoulders. Now, let's talk about manipulation.

The silent treatment feels powerful because it gives you control; it forces others to chase your attention. But that's not love; that's leverage. Emotional honesty doesn't play games. It doesn't make people earn access through guilt or confusion. If your silence is designed to make them anxious, that's not a boundary, that's bondage.

God never called you to be distant to prove a point. He called you to tell you the truth in love (Ephesians 4:15). Love communicates. Love corrects. Love listens. Silence that shames is not love, it's pride wearing perfume. You may think you're punishing them, but you're really punishing yourself. You miss opportunities for growth, connection, and understanding because pride won't let you speak. Every moment you stay silent to "win," you lose another chance for peace.

Emotional honesty means learning to say, "This conversation is hard for me," instead of shutting down completely. It's saying, "I need time, but I'm still committed to working through this." It's admitting that you're human, not hiding behind holiness. The Bible says in James 5:16 (NIV), *"Confess your sins to each other and pray for each other so that you may be healed."* You can't be healed in isolation.

Healing requires humility, and humility sounds like confession, not control. If you really want boundaries, build them with communication. Boundaries without conversation are just invisible walls, and people can't respect what they can't see. Be clear about what you need and why you need it. That's not weakness; that's wisdom. So, how do you relearn emotional honesty? You start by practicing honesty with God. Tell Him what you're afraid to say out loud. Tell Him who hurt you, who disappointed you, who makes your chest tighten when their name comes up.

The safest place to be vulnerable is in His presence. When you get used to being honest with God, you'll become more capable of being honest with people. And when you do speak, let your words be led by grace, not grief. You're not required to have every conversation, but you are called to handle relationships with righteousness. Silence may protect your pride, but honesty protects your peace.

Emotional honesty is scary, it demands vulnerability. But silence is scarier, because it demands isolation. You cannot claim to be emotionally mature while emotionally unavailable. So, the next time you feel tempted to disappear, remember this: distance may feel safe, but it's not always spiritual. And silence may feel powerful, but it's not always productive. Healing doesn't come from hiding; it comes from humility. If you want peace, talk it out. Pray it out. Cry it out. But whatever you do, don't shut down. Because every time you do, you mute not just people, but the very voice of healing that God is trying to release in your life.

You can't weaponize silence and call it wisdom. You can't build walls and call it discernment. And you can't live healed while using coldness as a coping mechanism. So, the next time you're tempted to withdraw and call it spiritual, ask yourself this question: Is this silence coming from peace, or from pain? Because one restores. The other rots.

⚷ FAITH PRESCRIPTION

When Silence Turns into Self-Protection Instead of Sanctification
So, let's be honest, your version of "being still and knowing" has looked a lot like ghosting people and calling it holiness. You've been fasting from conversation, not food. You've turned "guarding your heart" into a lifestyle of avoiding anyone who challenges you. But the Holy Spirit isn't impressed by your emotional cold front. He's calling you back into communication, compassion, and community. Here's your treatment plan. Take daily, no substitutions. Side effects may include humility, vulnerability, and unexpected peace.

1. Diagnose the Source of the Silence
Before you can fix it, you need to name it. Are you quiet because you're at peace, or because you're angry? Are you withdrawing

because you need time to heal, or because you want them to notice your absence? God never heals what we keep hiding under fake boundaries.

℞ **Scripture Dose:** *"Search me, God, and know my heart; test me and know my anxious thoughts."* Psalm 139:23 (NIV)

Practical Step: Ask yourself honestly: "What am I avoiding by staying silent?" Write it down. Bring it into prayer. God can't work with what you won't name.

2. Replace Punishment with Pause

There's nothing wrong with taking a break to breathe and process. But breaks have expiration dates; punishment doesn't. The next time you want to retreat, set a healthy time limit. Silence for reflection is medicine. Silence for manipulation is poison.

℞ **Scripture Dose:** *"There is a time for silence and a time to speak."* Ecclesiastes 3:7 (NIV)

Practical Step: Tell the person, "I need some time to pray and process. Let's talk in a few days." That's boundary, not bitterness. It gives space without creating separation.

3. <u>Communicate Before You Cut Off</u>

Most relationships don't die from betrayal; they die from avoidance. Saying nothing is not the same as saying everything's fine. God doesn't call us to be silent assassins; He calls us to be peacemakers.

℞ **Scripture Dose:** *"If your brother or sister sins against you, go and point out their fault, just between the two of you."* Matthew 18:15 (NIV)

Practical Step: Practice sentence starters that sound like honesty instead of hostility:
- "I value our relationship, but that conversation hurt."
- "I need clarity, not distance."

- "Let's talk when we can both listen." This is what maturity sounds like.

4. Break the Habit of Withholding

Every time you go silent to "teach someone a lesson," you teach yourself how to isolate. Withholding love, communication, or affection is emotional control, not spiritual discipline. God never withholds love to prove a point; neither should you.

℞ **Scripture Dose:** *"Freely you have received; freely give."* Matthew 10:8 (NIV)

Practical Step: When tempted to pull away, do the opposite, send a text, pray for them, or say a blessing. Don't let pride decide the temperature of your relationships.

5. Practice Confession Instead of Disappearing

When you're hurt, say so. When you're tired, say so. When you're overwhelmed, say so. Pretending you're fine while giving the cold shoulder is dishonesty with a halo on it. Confession keeps the heart unclogged.

℞ **Scripture Dose:** *"Confess your sins to each other and pray for each other so that you may be healed."* James 5:16 (NIV)

Practical Step: Tell God and at least one trusted friend, "I've been using silence as a defense. Help me change that." Healing always begins with honesty.

6. Redefine Boundaries the Biblical Way

Boundaries were never meant to keep people out of your life, only sin out of your space. A healthy boundary is an act of stewardship, not punishment. You can say "no" with grace and still be Christlike.

℞ **Scripture Dose:** *"Above all else, guard your heart, for everything you do flows from it."* Proverbs 4:23 (NIV)

Practical Step: Write out your boundaries, then add this phrase under each: "This is not a wall. It's a gate with love on both sides." That keeps your heart protected *and* open to reconciliation.

7. Invite the Holy Spirit into the Conversation

When your emotions are loud, let His presence speak first. Before you send that text, post that status, or start the "I'm done" speech, ask Him to translate your feelings into grace. The Holy Spirit is not silent; He's gentle.

℞ **Scripture Dose:** *"The Advocate, the Holy Spirit, will teach you all things and will remind you of everything I have said to you."* John 14:26 (NIV)

Practical Step: Whisper this before every hard talk: "Holy Spirit, teach me to respond, not react." It will change the entire atmosphere of your conversations.

8. Learn to Sit in Discomfort Without Disconnecting

Growth is uncomfortable. Conversations that heal are often the ones you want to avoid. Silence feels easier, but it steals intimacy. Jesus never avoided discomfort, He entered it to bring peace.

℞ **Scripture Dose:** *"Blessed are the peacemakers, for they will be called children of God."* Matthew 5:9 (NIV)

Practical Step: Stay in the room when it's awkward. Take a deep breath. Let empathy speak before ego. Remember, peacekeepers avoid conflict, but peacemakers redeem it.

9. Replace Coldness with Compassion

You don't need to harden your heart to protect it. Cold hearts feel nothing, but healed hearts feel wise. The Holy Spirit will teach you how to be soft and strong at the same time.

℞ **Scripture Dose:** *"Be kind and compassionate to one another, forgiving each other, just as in Christ God forgave you."* Ephesians 4:32 (NIV)

Practical Step: Instead of shutting down, pray this: "God, help me stay tender where life tried to make me tough."

10. Speak the Truth in Love, Then Rest

After you've prayed, processed, and spoken your peace, stop explaining. Silence isn't wrong when it's rooted in resolution. Say what needs to be said, then rest in God's approval, not theirs.

℞ **Scripture Dose:** *"Let your 'Yes 'be 'Yes, 'and your 'No,' 'No.'"* Matthew 5:37 (NIV)

Practical Step: When the conversation ends, don't replay it. Don't rewrite it. Rest. Silence after honesty is peace, not punishment.

Prescription Summary

Treatment	Dosage	Purpose
Self-examination	Daily	Exposes hidden motives behind silence
Communication	Regular	Build bridges instead of barriers
Confession	As needed	Keeps the heart clean
Compassion	Continuous	Replaces coldness with connection
Rest	Nightly	Teaches peace after honesty

📄 **Side Effects:** Softer tone, stronger boundaries, fewer grudges, and conversations that end in grace instead of guilt.

🕊 HOLY SPIRIT CONSULT

"You Can't Heal What You Keep Quiet About"
I've been watching the way you go quietly when you're hurt. You call it peace, but I know it's painful. You tell people you're fine, but your silence has become your shield, and your prison. I see the moments when you walk away mid-conversation, not because

you've found calm, but because you're afraid of confrontation. You've confused stillness with shutdown, and I want to teach you the difference.

Your silence feels safe because it gives you control. It keeps you from saying what you might regret, but it also keeps you from saying what could heal. You've learned to disappear instead of dealing. But children, avoiding communication doesn't protect your peace, it postpones your growth.

I never asked you to weaponize silence. I asked you to walk in peace. And peace doesn't punish; it restores. Every time you use distance to make someone feel your absence, you're stepping out of My flow. You can't freeze people out and expect My fire to stay alive in you. When I pull you into stillness, it's to quiet your spirit, not to close your heart. The kind of quiet I call you to brings clarity, not coldness. I want you to listen, not lock yourself away.

My stillness draws you closer to Me; your silence pushes people away from you. I know you're afraid of being misunderstood again. I know how deeply words have wounded you before. You think silence will keep you safe from rejection, but it's really keeping you from restoration. You've built walls and called them wisdom, but I'm ready to show you that wisdom looks like honesty covered in humility. You say you're setting boundaries, but sometimes you're building barriers. The line between them is thinner than you think. Boundaries are led by love; barriers are led by fear. I can use your voice to bring healing, but only if you stop using it to disappear.

When you shut down, you silence more than your emotions, you silence Me. I speak through conviction, through conversation, through courage, not through cold shoulders. I can't use a mouth that refuses to move. Do you remember when I said, "Let there be light"? Creation began with communication. Life responds to words, not withdrawal. That is why the enemy wants you to mute, because every time you choose silence out of pride, he wins another moment of distance between you and the ones I sent to love you.

Child, speak again. Even if your voice trembles. Even if your heart isn't ready. Even if the last time you tried, it didn't go well. I'm not asking you to be perfect, just present. Your silence may feel spiritual, but your voice carries My Spirit. Stop confusing withdrawal with wisdom. Stop mistaking avoidance for anointing. I didn't call you to hide from hard conversations; I called you to handle them differently. Speak truth but wrap it in gentleness. Set boundaries but keep compassion. Be quiet when it's for peace, not punishment. I know you think silence makes you strong, but vulnerability makes you whole. You can't heal what you keep quiet about. So, here's My prescription: Talk to Me first, then talk to them in love. And if you don't know what to say, I'll give you the words. Because real peace doesn't need distance, it needs direction.

📖 DECLARATIONS JOURNAL

"The Silent Treatment Isn't Spiritual Warfare"
Instructions : These declarations are medicine for a closed mouth and a guarded heart. Speak to them aloud until they sound like truth. Then write what the Holy Spirit reveals to you underneath each one.

💬 1. Declaration of Honesty

I will no longer hide behind silence and call it strength. God gave me a voice to build bridges, not walls. My peace doesn't require punishment, it requires presence. I am learning to speak the truth in love and let grace do the rest.

Reflection: What conversation have I been avoiding out of fear, pride, or pain?

____

____

____

⚕ 2. Declaration of Healing

I am not healed by distance; I am healed by honesty. Silence doesn't protect me; it isolates me. God is teaching me to process, not to punish. I will no longer withdraw to feel powerful. I will speak to grow peaceful.

Reflection: How has my silence hurt me or others more than it helped?

🌿 3. Declaration of Boundaries

My boundaries will be built with grace, not guilt. They will protect peace, not pride. I can say "no" with love and "yes" without fear. I don't need to disappear to feel safe; I just need to stay grounded in truth.

Reflection: What does a healthy boundary look like for me, one that honors God and people?

◉ 4. Declaration of Connection

I am done using silence to make others chase me. I will stop confusing control with care. I am capable of connection that doesn't compromise who I am. My relationships will reflect God's grace, honest, humble, and whole.

Reflection: What relationship have I frozen that God wants to thaw through communication?

____

____

____

⊞ 5. Declaration of Peace

I don't need to win the argument; I just need to keep my heart clean. Peace is not the absence of noise, it is the presence of God. When I choose honesty over avoidance, I honor the One who healed me. Today, I speak, with love, with courage, and without fear.

Reflection: How can I practice peace this week without hiding behind silence?

____

____

____

🕊 **Final Note:** Your silence may have felt like control, but it was really captivity. Let your words become worship again, not noise, but truth. God isn't asking for perfect communication. He's asking for participation.

A Prayer for Reclaiming My Voice and Releasing My Walls
Father, I come to You today with my mouth closed but my heart loud. You know the words I haven't said, the ones that sit in my chest like a knot, the words that come with tears, pride, and a fear of being misunderstood again. You see the silence I've been hiding behind. You know when it's peaceful and when it's punishment.

God, I confess that I've used my silence as a weapon. I've gone quietly to make people feel what I felt, the rejection, confusion, the sting of being ignored. I told myself it was maturity, but really, it was control. I called it "guarding my peace," but I was just guarding my pain. Forgive me for pretending my silence was spiritual when it was selfish.

I see now that silence can become a stronghold when pride sits in the driver's seat. I've punished people for not understanding me instead of helping them understand. I've walked away when I should have stayed long enough to talk it through. I've chosen distance because it felt easier than humility. But Lord, I don't want to be right anymore, I want to be healed.

Teach me how to speak again, not to argue, not to defend, but to build. Give me courage to say what's true and grace to say it with gentleness. Let my words carry healing instead of hostility. When I'm tempted to retreat, remind me that You didn't design me for isolation, You designed me for connection.

Father, remind me that communication is part of Your image in me. You spoke creation into being. You sent Your Word to heal. You talk with me daily through Your Spirit. Help me reflect that same heart in my relationships. When I'm afraid of confrontation, I remind myself that confrontation done in love is not chaos, it's clarity.

God, I surrender the pride that makes me want to prove a point instead of pursue peace. I release the fear that convinces me to hide instead of healing. Help me stop disappearing when things get uncomfortable. Let my silence become sacred, not manipulative. Let my pauses be for prayer, not punishment. Heal the part of me that still thinks love means pretending nothing's wrong. Heal the part of me that still associates vulnerability with weakness. Healing the part of me that thinks being distant makes me strong.

Fill me with Your Spirit so deeply that even my tone sounds like grace. Teach me to listen without defensiveness, to speak without resentment, and to pause without pride. May every conversation I have reflect Your presence, not my pain. And Lord, for every relationship I've damaged with my silence, open the door for restoration. Give me discernment to know when to reach out and humility to do it without conditions. Where my silence has created confusion, give me the words that bring clarity. Where it has caused distance, let reconciliation start with me.

*God, I want my boundaries to protect my peace, not my bitterness. Help me build them with compassion, not coldness. Help me use my voice like You, firm but loving, honest but kind. From this day forward, may my silence serve You, not my pride. May my stillness reflect Your Spirit, not my stubbornness. May my voice bring healing, not hurt. You didn't create me to vanish. You created me to reflect Your voice, steady, truthful, and full of life. So today, I will speak again. In Jesus 'name, **Amen.***

REFLECTION PAGE

"The Silent Treatment Isn't Spiritual Warfare"

Date: _______________________________

Patient Name: _______________________________

♡ **Heart Check:** Am I truly at peace, or am I just avoiding the person or situation that challenges me?

____

____

⚕ **Spiritual X-Ray:** When I go silent, what emotion am I really trying to manage, fear, pride, anger, or exhaustion?

____

____

____

____

🌿 **Treatment Plan:** What would healthy honesty look like in my next difficult conversation?

____

____

____

____

____

💧 **Faith Declaration:** "God, I refuse to weaponize my silence. Let my words bring healing, my pauses bring peace, and my heart stay open, even when it hurts."

____

____

____

____

____

Discharge Note: Silence isn't always holy, sometimes it's just hiding. This week, I will speak when God says speak and be still when He says *he still.*

Signature: __________________________________

Date: __________________________________

Reflections

____

____

____

____

____

____

____

____

____

____

Chapter 6:
Forgiving People Who Don't Even Feel Bad

◆ SYMPTOM:
Internal rage dressed in self-righteous calm.

You've mastered the art of looking unbothered. You smile at the person who betrayed you. You even greet them at church, nod politely, maybe even say, "God bless you," while your insides are screaming, *"I hope the Wi-Fi goes out during your favorite show."* Outwardly, you look composed, calm, collected, sanctified. But deep down, you're boiling. You've just learned how to mask your anger with Christian manners.

Your calm isn't peaceful, it's performance. You've traded outbursts for appearances. You don't explode anymore; you simmer quietly under the surface, convincing yourself that because you didn't lash out, you've forgiven them. But forgiveness isn't measured by how well you hide your fury; it is measured by how fully you've surrendered your right to revenge. You've built an altar to your restraint. You pat yourself on the back for not clapping back. You tell yourself, *"I'm more mature now; I just let God handle it."* But the truth is, you're not letting God handle it, you're just watching to see how He does it. You want to witness their downfall so you can whisper, "That's what happens when you mess with me."

You've mistaken silence for sanctification. You don't yell anymore, but you rehearse every scenario in your head, what you should've said, what you wish you'd done, how you'd have handled it *if you weren't trying to be holy.* You're having full-blown arguments in your imagination, and God's like, "You're still fighting battles that ended three seasons ago."

This kind of bitterness is quiet but deadly. It doesn't shout. It smiles. It's polite. It shows up to worship night, lifts its hands, and sings about freedom, all while gripping invisible grudges. You've convinced yourself that you've forgiven them because you've stopped talking about it, but forgiveness isn't silence, it's release.

Let's be honest, some people don't even look sorry. They're out here living their best life, unbothered, posting scriptures on Instagram, while you're still trying to keep your jaw from clenching every time their name comes up. You keep wondering why God hasn't convicted them yet. You're like, "Lord, did You not see what they did?" And God's like, "Yes, I did, and now I'm trying to see what *you'll* do."

You've dressed up your rage in spiritual clothing. You pray for them, but your prayers sound suspiciously like curses wrapped in King James English: "Lord, deal with them according to their deeds." You say you've let it go, but every time someone brings them up, you say, "Oh, I'm fine," with a tone that says you're anything but. You're walking around with what I call "holy hostility" the kind that hides behind politeness and Scripture quotes. You're too saved to explode but too angry to heal. And the most dangerous part? You think your composure is spiritual progress. But calm without cleansing is just control. The enemy loves this version of you, composed but cold, polite but poisoned. You think you're protecting your peace, but you're really preserving your pain. You're not free; you're just functioning with a spiritual limp that you call maturity. You're like a patient refusing physical therapy, the wound's closed, but you can't move right.

Forgiveness isn't about pretending it didn't hurt. It's about refusing to let it harden your heart. And the truth is, some of the people who hurt you will *never* feel bad about it. They won't apologize. They won't admit what they did. They may even twist the story to make it look like you were the problem. And that's when forgiveness gets real, because it's no longer about their repentance, it's about your release. The hardest kind of forgiveness is the one that has no audience. No apology. No closure. Just you and God, standing over the ashes of what they destroyed, deciding that bitterness won't get the last word. That's the kind of forgiveness that heaven applauds, the kind no one claps for, but angels record.

But here's the truth you need to face you can't heal from what you keep rehearsing. You can't let go while still checking their life for divine payback. You can't move forward while dragging their memory like an emotional security blanket. And you can't walk in freedom while praying for their failure.

Forgiveness doesn't mean you trust them again. It doesn't mean you excuse what happened. It means you refuse to let their offense become your identity. Because if you're not careful, you'll start building your personality around your pain, everything you do, say, and believe will orbit what they did to you.

Bitterness will convince you that being angry keeps you safe. It'll whisper, *"Don't forgive, they'll just do it again."* But forgiveness isn't about them. It's about freeing yourself from the emotional leash they left around your heart. And yes, it's unfair. They hurt you and get to walk around fine. They broke your trust and act like it never happened. But God never said forgiveness would feel fair, He said it would make you free. So, here's the real diagnosis: you're still angry, but you've learned to make it look holy. You've turned resentment into routine. You quote "Let go and let God," but deep down you're just hoping He lets you watch. And the Holy Spirit is gently saying, "I need you to stop performing peace and start pursuing it."

Forgiveness isn't weakness; it's warfare. It's how you fight without losing your soul. It's how you say, "You don't owe me anything anymore, because Jesus already paid for it." The question isn't whether they feel bad. The question is whether you're ready to be free.

℞ TEACHING

How Jesus modeled forgiveness without audience or applause, and how that frees your faith.

When Jesus was hanging on the cross, His final words weren't, "Wait until they apologize." He said, *"Father, forgive them, for they know not what they do."* (Luke 23:34, NIV). No public confrontation. No dramatic moment of reconciliation. Just raw mercy in the middle of mockery. That is the blueprint.

Forgiveness, according to Jesus, doesn't require acknowledgment, it requires alignment. You align your heart with heaven even when earth refuses to make sense. You choose mercy over memory. And you release what justice can't fix.

Most people want to forgive, but they also want witnesses. They want the person to admit their wrongs in front of an audience, so everyone knows who was right. But Jesus modeled forgiveness in private pain. He forgave in isolation, not applause. That's the maturity that frees your faith, when your healing isn't dependent on their humility. You see, forgiveness is less about others and more about obedience. It's not emotional amnesia; it's spiritual authority. It says, "I refuse to let what they did rob me of what God is doing." When you forgive, you reclaim your power, not by winning, but by releasing.

Let's be clear, forgiveness doesn't make what they did okay. It makes *you* okay. It doesn't erase the offense; it erases its ownership over you. The devil's favorite tool isn't temptation; it's torment through remembrance. If he can keep you playing the highlight reel of their offense, he can keep you distracted from your assignment.

Ephesians 4:31–32 (NIV) says, *"Get rid of all bitterness, rage and anger, brawling and slander, along with every form of malice. Be kind and compassionate to one another, forgiving each other, just as in Christ God forgave you."* Notice that: *get rid of it.* Not "wait until they apologize." Not "pray until you feel ready." Just *get rid of it.* Because forgiveness isn't a feeling; it is a choice.
If you wait until you feel ready to forgive, you'll die waiting. Forgiveness is an act of faith, a declaration that God's justice is better than your version of revenge. It's saying, "I trust You to handle what I can't heal."

Jesus didn't forgive because they deserved it. He forgave because He was determined to fulfill His purpose. If He had waited for people to "feel bad," the cross would've never happened. Some of your greatest callings will require you to forgive people who will never see their wrongs. That's not a weakness, that's walking in resurrection power.

Forgiveness is what keeps you from becoming the thing that hurts you. It stops you from passing down pain to the next person, from poisoning your prayers with pride, and from turning worship into warfare against people who may never even think of you again.

You may never get an apology, but you can still get peace. You can still grow. You can still thrive. Because forgiveness doesn't change the past, it changes what the past does to you. So how do you do it? You stop waiting for their remorse. You stop checking their life to see if karma worked. You stop letting their name trigger your trauma. And you start talking to God like this: "Lord, I forgive them, not because they've earned it, but because I refuse to carry what You already nailed to the cross." When you forgive yourself like that, your prayers start sounding different. You no longer ask God to expose them; you ask Him to expand you. You no longer beg for revenge, you ask for restoration. Because forgiveness doesn't just heal your heart; it grows your faith. You begin to trust God deeper when you release what justice can't repair. You learn that God's silence in their judgment isn't neglect, it's grace. And the same grace that covers them is the grace that's been covering you all along.

Jesus didn't wait for applause to extend mercy. He forgave out of alignment, not attention. That's where your freedom lives, in the quiet, uncelebrated places where you decide to let go before they ever feel bad. You don't forgive because they deserve peace. You forgive because *you* do.

💊 FAITH PRESCRIPTION

When Forgiveness Feels Like Losing, But It's Actually Freedom
Let's be honest, forgiving someone who doesn't even feel bad feels like handing them a trophy they didn't earn. You want them to hurt like you did. You want them to understand. You want them to at least *look* sorry. But here is the hard truth: your healing can't depend on their remorse. Because if your forgiveness needs their apology, you've handed them control of your peace.

Forgiveness is not approval. It's release. It's saying, "You can go, I'm done letting your offense live rent-free in my spirit." You're not freeing them from accountability; you're freeing yourself from the emotional lease of their memory. Here's your prescription plan, designed by heaven, delivered through grace.

1. Stop Waiting for Them to Feel It
Some people will never feel sorry because conviction requires humility, and humility requires honesty. If they can't face their own reflection, don't make it your mission to hold the mirror.

℞ **Scripture Dose:** *"Father, forgive them, for they know not what they do."* Luke 23:34 (NIV)

Practical Step: Say it out loud, "They may never feel bad, but I refuse to feel bound." You can't live healed while hoping they'll wake up one day and realize what they lost.

2. Trade Justice for Joy

You want payback. You want to see them reap what they sowed. But God's justice doesn't operate on your timeline, and that's a mercy to *both* of you. Every moment you spend waiting for revenge is a moment peace could be working if you'd just let it.

℞ **Scripture Dose:** *"Do not repay anyone evil for evil... Do not take revenge, my dear friends, but leave room for God's wrath."* Romans 12:17, 19 (NIV)

Practical Step: When bitterness rises, pray: "God, replace my obsession with fairness with an obsession for freedom." Because you can't heal while replaying someone else's judgment reel.

3. Redefine Forgiveness

Forgiveness doesn't mean pretending. It doesn't mean what they did was okay. It means you refuse to let it define your future. It's choosing not to make your pain your personality.

℞ **Scripture Dose:** *"Bear with each other and forgive one another... Forgive as the Lord forgave you."* Colossians 3:13 (NIV)

Practical Step: Write down what the situation stole from you, your trust, your peace, your sleep, your joy, and then pray over each one, asking God to restore it. Forgiveness is how you take it all back.

4. Refuse to Perform Forgiveness

There's fake forgiveness, the kind that smiles in public and seethes in private. It looks holy but sounds bitter when you talk about it. Real forgiveness doesn't need an audience; it just needs honesty.

♱ **Scripture Dose:** *"When you stand praying, if you hold anything against anyone, forgive them, so that your Father in heaven may forgive you."* Mark 11:25 (NIV)

Practical Step: Ask yourself, "Would my forgiveness still stand if no one knew I offered it?" Forgiveness that requires attention isn't freedom, it's performance.

5. Remember: You've Been Forgiven, Too
We all want grace for ourselves and justice for everyone else. But Jesus tied your forgiveness to how you forgive others, not to punish you, but to remind you that mercy is a flow, not a trophy.

♱ **Scripture Dose:** *"Forgive us our debts, as we also have forgiven our debtors."* Matthew 6:12 (NIV)

Practical Step: Every time you think of what they did, whisper "I've done worse, and God forgave me." Not to excuse their sin, but to remember the size of your Savior.

6. Release the Fantasy Version of Justice
You keep picturing that perfect scene, the day they finally come crawling back, tears in their eyes, begging for forgiveness. But every time you imagine that you're still living in bondage. The fantasy of their apology is keeping your heart in captivity.

♱ **Scripture Dose:** *"You will keep in perfect peace those whose minds are steadfast, because they trust in you."* Isaiah 26:3 (NIV)

Practical Step: Replace that fantasy scene with this prayer: "Lord, I trust You to handle their conviction and my healing." That shift changes everything.

7. Let God Be the One Who Balances the Scale
Bitterness is your attempt to play accountant with God's justice, constantly checking if the math adds up. But He doesn't settle accounts the way you do. His goal isn't revenge; it's redemption.

℞ **Scripture Dose:** *"The Lord will fight for you; you need only to be still."* Exodus 14:14 (NIV)

Practical Step: Write this on your mirror: "God handles justice better than I handle joy." Then watch your perspective change every morning.

8. Forgive Without Announcement

You don't have to post about it, tell them, or prove it. True forgiveness is internal work that produces external peace. Sometimes you'll know you've forgiven them because their name no longer hijacks your emotions.

℞ **Scripture Dose:** *"Love keeps no record of wrongs."* 1 Corinthians 13:5 (NIV)

Practical Step: Each time their name crosses your mind, say: "God, bless them, and keep working on me." That's how bitterness dies, through blessings whispered in faith.

9. Let Forgiveness Free Your Faith

Unforgiveness is like spiritual cholesterol, it clogs the arteries of your faith. It blocks answered prayer, clear hearing, and peace. Forgiveness isn't optional if you want spiritual flow.

℞ **Scripture Dose:** *"If you forgive other people when they sin against you, your heavenly Father will also forgive you."* Matthew 6:14 (NIV)

Practical Step: Before praying for anything new, release anything old. "God, before I ask for more, help me release what's still stuck." Faith flows better through a clean heart.

10. Don't Confuse Forgiveness with Reconciliation

Forgiveness is your responsibility. Reconciliation is a joint effort. Sometimes God calls you to release people completely, not to restore what was, but to restore who you are.

℞ **Scripture Dose:** *"As far as it depends on you, live at peace with everyone."* Romans 12:18 (NIV)

Practical Step: You can forgive fully and still set boundaries wisely. Write this in your journal: "Forgiveness doesn't reopen doors; it removes the locks from my heart."

Prescription Summary

Treatment	Dosage	Purpose
Forgiveness	Daily	Prevents spiritual heart failure
Gratitude	Morning	Refocuses faith on grace, not grievance
Prayer	As needed	Replaces revenge with release
Reflection	Weekly	Checks emotional health progress
Boundaries	Continuous	Keeps peace sustainable

📖 **Side Effects:** Unexplainable calm, emotional maturity, the ability to see their name without tightening your jaw, and a sudden realization that peace was worth more than pride all along.

🕊 HOLY SPIRIT CONSULT

"You're Still Waiting for Sorry, But I'm Waiting for Surrender."
I know you're tired of pretending you're over it. You've said all the right words, "I've forgiven them," "I'm moving on," "It's in God's hands" but deep down, you're still waiting. Waiting for them to feel what you felt. Waiting for the apology that finally validates your pain. Waiting for justice looks like humiliation. But here's what I need you to hear: you can't heal while waiting for someone else to

feel. Your freedom doesn't depend on their remorse. It depends on your release.

You think letting go means they win. But forgiveness isn't losing, it's leaving. It's walking out of the emotional prison you've decorated with scripture and called "boundaries." You've been standing guard over your pain for so long that you forgot I came to take the shift. Yes, they hurt you. Yes, they acted like nothing happened. And yes, I saw all the betrayal, gossip, disregard, manipulation. I saw the text they sent, the rumors they started, the trust they broke. But I didn't just see what they did to you; I see what it's doing to you now.

You smile in public, but I see the reply in private. You tell others, "I'm fine," but your heart still races when their name pops up. You've built peace around avoidance instead of My presence. And I need you to understand something: peace built on pretending isn't peace at all. It's paralysis.

You've prayed for Me to deal with them, but I've been trying to deal with you. You've been asking Me to convict their heart, but I've been whispering to yours: *"Let Me have it."* Let Me have the bitterness. Let Me have imaginary revenge. Let Me have the conversations you keep having in your head. Let Me have the justice you keep demanding in your prayers. Child, I know it feels unfair. I know you think forgiving them lets them off too easily. But forgiveness was never about letting them go free, it was about freeing you from becoming like them.

You think holding onto anger protects you, but it's poisoning you. Every time you rehearse the offense, you reopen the wound I'm trying to heal. You keep asking Me to make them see how wrong they were, but what if I'm using this moment to show you how right I want your heart to be? You don't have to understand their motives to forgive their actions. You don't need to choose compassion. You don't need them to feel guilty before you release grace. Because forgiveness isn't fairness, it's faith. It's trusting that I saw, I remember, and I will handle it in ways you never could.

Do you know why Jesus said, *"Father, forgive them"* and not *"I forgive them"*? Because even He understood that true forgiveness flows from the Father's heart. You can't manufacture it; you can only surrender to it. So, stop trying to convince yourself you've forgiven them. Just ask Me to do it through you. And when you see them, smiling, succeeding, unbothered, don't let bitterness tell you that I've forgotten justice. Grace doesn't cancel consequences; it just shifts the focus from punishment to purpose. My timing is perfect, even when it's quiet.

I need you to release them for real this time. Not in a post. Not in a prayer, you half-believe. But in your heart. I need you to stop stalking their progress and start stewarding your peace. I need you to forgive even when it doesn't make sense, because that's when forgiveness works best, when it's unreasonable.

You can't follow Me while dragging the ghosts of your offenders behind you. Every ounce of energy you spend waiting for them to feel bad is energy you could be using to step into what's next. So let them go. Not because they deserve it, but because you deserve to breathe again. Let them go, not to erase the past, but to protect your future. Let them go, because I'm still writing your story, and they were only a chapter. I know this hurts, but I promise you, forgiveness won't kill you. Bitterness will. So, child... hand Me the file you've been keeping on them.

Stop building your peace around their pain. Stop waiting for "sorry" when I've already said, "It's finished." You don't need closure when the cross has already closed it.

📖 DECLARATIONS JOURNAL

"Forgiving People Who Don't Even Feel Bad"
Instructions : Speak these declarations aloud until your spirit starts to agree, even if your emotions don't yet. Forgiveness is not a feeling; it's a decision that rewires your heart one word at a time.

✚ 1. Declaration of Freedom

I forgive them, not because they apologized, but because I refuse to carry them another day. Their silence no longer controls my peace. I am not waiting for "sorry" when Jesus already said, "It is finished." Forgiveness isn't weakness; it's proof that grace runs deeper than grief.

Reflection: Who am I still carrying that God has already called me to release?

____

____

____

____

💬 2. Declaration of Perspective

I may never understand why they did what they did, but I trust that God can use it to shape who I'm becoming. The story isn't over just because they didn't repent. God can write redemption into what they meant for ruin.

Reflection: How has this pain shaped me, and what is God still writing through it?

____

____

____

____

🩺 3. Declaration of Mercy

I will stop expecting remorse from those who don't feel it. Their lack of conviction does not cancel my calling. I will not wait for justice to move forward in joy. I will forgive quickly, because freedom is too expensive to delay.

Reflection: What does it look like to forgive quickly, even when it feels unfair?

____

____

____

____

🌿 4. Declaration of Peace

My healing no longer depends on their humility. Peace is not the product of their apology, it is the promise of God's presence. I release the fantasy of closure and choose the reality of calm. I will breathe again, live again, and love again, without bitterness.

Reflection: What does peace look like to me if the apology never comes?

____

____

____

____

💧 5. Declaration of Restoration

I may never get back what they took, but I will recover what I lost. God restores joy faster than bitterness steals it. Every time I forgive, I make room for blessing. My peace is proof that God won.

Reflection: What blessings have I seen (or expect to see) on the other side of forgiveness?

____

____

____

____

🕊 **Final Note:** Forgiveness doesn't make them right; it makes you ready. Ready for peace. Ready for healing. Ready for freedom. You are not weak in letting go. You are wise enough to stop bleeding for what's already been buried.

🙏 **GUIDED PRAYER**

A Prayer for Releasing the Unapologetic and Recovering My Peace
Father, you see what I'm still carrying. You see the names that tighten my chest, the memories that replay without warning, the anger that hides beneath my calm. I've said I've forgiven them, but You and I both know there's still a knot in my heart that won't untangle. I've been waiting for them to feel bad, to apologize to finally understand what they did to me. But they don't. And maybe they never will. So, here I am again, Lord, standing between what I want and what You've commanded. You told me to forgive, even when it's unfair. You told me to release it, even when it still hurts. You told me to love my enemies and pray for those who mistreat me, and sometimes I wonder if You really meant them. But deep down, I know You did.

God, I confess, I've been holding onto silent anger while calling it closure. I've wanted justice that looked like their humiliation. I've prayed "righteous" prayers that were really revenge in disguise. Forgive me for wanting their pain more than Your peace. Forgive me for trying to make myself judge, jury, and executioner over someone You've already placed under grace.

I don't understand how You could forgive people who never even said they were sorry. I don't understand how You could hang on a cross and say, "Father, forgive them," while they mocked You. But I want to learn that kind of strength, the kind that looks weak to the world but wins in heaven.

Lord, I release them, every person who lied, betrayed, rejected, or used me. I release the ones who acted like it never happened. I release the ones who blamed me for their actions. I release the ones who pretend they're healed while I'm still working through the wreckage. I can't keep carrying them anymore.

They don't owe me an apology, because You already gave me an answer: "It is finished." You paid for my peace when they forfeited theirs. You redeemed my story when they refused responsibility. So, I let go, not because they deserve it, but because You deserve my obedience.

Heal the part of me that still needs them to feel something. Heal the part of me that thinks I can't move forward until they do. Heal the part of me that equates fairness with freedom. Help me stop checking if they're miserable and start checking if I'm growing. Lord, every time bitterness tries to rise again, reminds me that I'm not them, and I don't have to become them to prove my worth. When I'm tempted to replay the conversation, silence the scene with Your peace. When I want to retaliate, I remind myself of the mercy that once covered me.

I choose to forgive, fully, freely, and finally. Not halfway. Not conditionally. Not with resentment disguised as maturity. I forgive so I can live again. I forgive you so I can breathe again. I forgive so You can fill the spaces I've been keeping blocked off with pride and pain. And God, if forgiveness is a process, then walk with me through every step. When it resurfaces tomorrow, help me release it again. When the memory stings next month, remind me that healing takes time, but bitterness only takes agreement.

Today, I chose You over revenge. I choose peace over punishment. I choose joy over justice. I choose to forgive people who don't even feel bad, because I finally understand that this forgiveness isn't about them, it's about me, healed and whole in You. So here it is, God, all the weight I've carried, all the pain I've managed, all the justice I've tried to control. It's Yours now. All of it. In Jesus 'name, **Amen.**

REFLECTION PAGE

"Forgiving People Who Don't Even Feel Bad"
Date: _______________________________
Patient Name: _______________________________

💭 **Heart Check:** What emotion do I still feel when I think about the person who hurt me, peace, anger, sadness, or indifference?

____

____

____

____

____

____

____

⚕ **Spiritual Diagnosis:** Am I waiting for an apology, or am I willing to move forward without one?

____

____

____

____

🌿 **Treatment Plan:** What practical step can I take this week to walk in forgiveness, prayer, release, or reconciliation?

____

____

____

____

____

____

____

____

Faith Declaration: "God, I forgive them, not because they asked, but because I'm ready to be free. Your justice is better than my judgment, and Your peace is better than my proof."

Discharge Note: Forgiveness doesn't always feel fair, but freedom always feels better than bitterness. I'm walking out lighter, not because they changed, but because *I did.*

Signature: _______________________________

Date: _________________________________

Reflections

Chapter 7:
The Parent Trap, When Guilt Breeds Resentment

⬤ SYMPTOM: Feeling unappreciated, unseen, or exhausted by your own children.

You love them, that's not the problem. The problem is that lately, love feels more like labor. You wake up every day giving, guiding, teaching, correcting, praying, feeding, driving, paying, and somehow still ending the night wondering, *Do they even see me?*

You don't say it out loud because it sounds unholy to admit you're bitter toward your kids. Parents aren't supposed to feel that way. You're supposed to love unconditionally, right? But you've started noticing the resentment in your sighs, the irritation in your patience, and the guilt in your silence. You feel drained, emotionally, spiritually, financially, and you're running on fumes, telling yourself that it's just "a busy season," but it's really a bitter one.

You've mastered the art of the "I'm fine" smile while silently counting how many times you've been taken for granted. They call your name 47 times in an hour, but you can't remember the last time they said thank you. You bend, stretch, and sacrifice daily, but there's a quiet ache growing, the kind that whispers, *"What about me?"*

It is the hidden anger of the overworked and the overlooked. The parent who shows up but feels unseen. You pray for patience, but if one more person leaves their plate in the sink, you're about to quote scripture with the passion of a prophet in crisis. And then comes the guilt. Because the moment you feel the bitterness rise, you shame yourself for it. You say, *"They're just kids."* You remind yourself of all the parents who would give anything to have children. You remember that parenting is a gift, but right now, it feels more like a grind.

You love your children fiercely, but the exhaustion is real. You start avoiding moments that used to bring joy. You say, "I need a break," but you never take one because you're afraid of being called selfish. You feel guilty for wanting space, but you also feel resentful for never getting it.

This is the emotional loop so many parents live in, guilt feed resentment, resentment feeds the guilt, and both keep you too tired to heal. You can't pour from an empty cup, but you also can't refill it if you never stop pouring. Somewhere between diaper changes and college tuition, between carpools and parent-teacher conferences, your identity got tangled in their needs. You forgot that you're more than who they call "Mom" or "Dad." You've lost pieces of yourself while managing everyone else's life. And that loss? It festers.

Resentment creeps in when gratitude dries up, on both sides. You start to feel like they owe you appreciation, while they start assuming your love is endless and unconditional. But love without limits becomes labor without rest, and eventually, something breaks. You start snapping over small things. Not because the milk spilled, but because you're spilling over emotionally. You hear yourself using a tone that surprises even you. You tell them to go to their room, but part of you want to go to yours and not come out for a week.

Parenting from bitterness feels like walking on emotional eggshells. You give, but it's strained. You love it, but it's laced with weariness. You start measuring your worth by their behavior, if they're happy, you're doing well. If they struggle, you blame yourself. It is a trap, not the kind your kids  set, but the one guilt built. And the truth is, most of your anger isn't even about them. It's about you, the version of yourself that you sacrificed to raise them. The hobbies you put down. The dreams you delayed. The nights you stayed awake while everyone else slept. You've spent so long being their covering that you forgot you need one, too. But here's the secret no one wants to say out loud: even good parents can get bitter. Even loving parents can resent their role when they're unhealed, and under-rested. It doesn't make you ungrateful it makes you human.

Bitterness builds slowly, disguised as fatigue and frustration. It tells you, "You're doing all this for nothing." It convinces you that no one cares that your kids don't notice that your sacrifices are invisible. And if you don't deal with that voice, it starts shaping how you see them, not as blessings, but as burdens. You don't want to feel this way. You love them more than words could ever say. But you also want to feel like more than a 24-hour emotional support system. You want to breathe without guilt. You want joy without exhaustion. You want to look at your children without the weight of resentment coloring your affection. And that's where God meets you, not in your perfection, but in your depletion. He's not judging your exhaustion; He's inviting you to rest.

🩺 TEACHING

How bitterness poisons parenting and how grace restores the joy of nurturing again.

Bitterness in parenting doesn't happen overnight. It builds quietly in the background, collecting over years of giving without being filled, forgiving without being thanked, and showing up without being seen. It grows when we confuse self-sacrifice with self-erasure. And before you know it, you're doing everything right but feeling everything wrong.

The truth is that bitterness is the smoke that rises when the fire of joy burns out. Parenting through bitterness is like driving with fogged-up windows, you're moving, but you can't see clearly. Every little frustration feels bigger, every mistake feels personal, and every correction sounds like rejection.

God never designed parenting to drain you. He designed it to refine you. But when guilt and exhaustion take over, you start parenting from obligation instead of overflow. You stop nurturing souls and start managing behaviors. You start reacting to your kids instead of relating to them. And that's how bitterness poisons the home, one sigh, one eye roll, one emotional withdrawal at a time.

Ephesians 6:4 (NIV) says, *"Do not exasperate your children; instead, bring them up in the training and instruction of the Lord."* Notice it doesn't just tell kids to obey; it tells parents to watch their tone. Because frustration in the heart of a parent can suffocate the growth in the heart of a child.

The enemy doesn't have to destroy your family to disrupt it, he just needs to exhaust it. When parents get weary, distance grows. When guilt takes over, grace takes a back seat. And when bitterness festers, love becomes conditional, not intentionally, but emotionally. But here's what grace does: it rewires the whole thing. Grace reminds you that you're not their savior, you're their steward. You don't have to be perfect to be present. You don't have to do it all to do it well. Grace restores what guilt is distorted.

Grace says: "You're doing your best, and that's enough." "It's okay to rest before you react." "You can love your children without losing yourself." Grace frees you to forgive yourself for the moments you weren't patient, for the days you raised your voice, for the times you felt like running away. Grace reminds you that God isn't grading your parenting. He's guiding it. When you let bitterness go, joy comes back, not in big, dramatic ways, but in sacred, simple ones. In laughter over dinner. In bedtime prayers that don't feel rushed. In looking at your child and seeing a soul instead of a to-do list.

Parenting through grace also means letting your children see your humanity. You don't have to pretend you have it all together. In fact, your humility teaches them more about God than your perfection ever could. When they see you apologize, when they see you pray through frustration, when they see you choose gentleness over judgment, that's when they learn what love looks like in motion.

Bitterness tells you that your kids owe you something. Grace reminds you that your children were never debtors, they were entrusted with gifts. You're not raising servants; you're raising souls. And when you release the expectation that they must constantly validate your effort, you'll rediscover the joy of nurturing again.

Psalm 127:3 (NIV) says, *"Children are a heritage from the Lord, offspring a reward from him."* That word "heritage" means inheritance, not inconvenience. God entrusted them to you not to drain you, but to develop both of you. You're growing just as much as they are, in patience, in compassion, in dependence on Him.

So, take a deep breath. You're not failing because you feel tired, you're failing only if you stop bringing that tiredness to God. You can love deeply and still need rest. You can be grateful and still be honest about being exhausted. God isn't condemning your fatigue; He's inviting you to refill your cup.

Your kids don't need a perfect parent. They need a healed one. They need a mom or dad who loves out of grace, not guilt. They need someone who can model forgiveness, not just toward them, but toward themselves. So today, forgive yourself. Forgive them for being human. And forgive the idea that you're supposed to get it all right all the time. Parenting isn't about perfection, it's about presence. And where bitterness once poisoned, grace will water again.

💊 FAITH PRESCRIPTION

"When Guilt Pretends to Be Love and Bitterness Masquerades as Boundaries."

Parenting is one of the greatest blessings God gives, but if you're not careful, guilt will twist that blessing into a burden. The moment you start believing that exhaustion equals love, you step into a spiritual trap where resentment hides behind responsibility. You think, *"I'm doing everything I can,"* but your heart whispers, *"And it's still not enough."* That's not God's parenting plan; that's guilt's manipulation plan. God never designed parenthood to feel like punishment. He designed it to grow both you *and* them through grace. Here's how you start healing the fatigue and reclaiming joy in your role.

1. Admit the Bitterness Before It Multiplies

You can't heal what you hide behind "I'm fine." Bitterness in parenting isn't just yelling, sometimes it's silent detachment. You stop engaging, you stop laughing, you stop seeing them as individuals and start seeing them as responsibilities.

℞ **Scripture Dose:** *"See to it that no bitter root grows up to cause trouble and defile many."* Hebrews 12:15 (NIV)

Practical Step: Whisper this prayer: "Lord, show me where frustration has hardened into resentment." Write down one area where you've felt bitter and invite God to turn that into compassion.

2. Stop Parenting from Guilt

You over-give because you're overcompensating. You say yes when you want to say no. You punish yourself for not being perfect. But guilt-driven parenting produces exhaustion, not empathy.

℞ **Scripture Dose:** *"There is now no condemnation for those who are in Christ Jesus."* Romans 8:1 (NIV)

Practical Step: Before saying yes, ask yourself, *"Am I doing this from love or from guilt?"* If it's guilt, pause. God doesn't bless what burns you out.

3. Redefine Rest as Responsibility

You think resting makes you lazy, but in God's design, rest is obedience. When you rest, you reset your emotions. Jesus took naps, not because He was weak, but because He was wise.

℞ **Scripture Dose:** *"Come to me, all you who are weary and burdened, and I will give you rest."* Matthew 11:28 (NIV)

Practical Step: Schedule guilt-free rest. Literally write it on the calendar. "Rest" is not a luxury, it is a lifeline.

4. Replace Control with Compassion

You're not their savior. You can guide your children, but you can't guard them from every mistake. The tighter you grip, the faster joy slips away. Control drains. Compassion restores.

℞ **Scripture Dose:** *"As a father has compassion on his children, so the Lord has compassion on those who fear him."* Psalm 103:13 (NIV)

Practical Step: When you feel yourself getting to control, breathe and say: "God, You love them more than I do." Then step back. You can't be the Holy Spirit in their story.

5. Trade "Perfect Parent" Syndrome for Presence

You keep comparing yourself to other parents, the ones on Instagram with chore charts and smiling kids. Stop. Comparison breeds resentment faster than chaos breeds crumbs. Your kids don't need picture-perfect; they need peace filled.

℞ **Scripture Dose:** *"My grace is sufficient for you, for my power is made perfect in weakness."* 2 Corinthians 12:9 (NIV)

Practical Step: Every time you feel inadequate, say: "Grace covers what guilt condemns." "Then spend five minutes being *fully present*, no phone, no pressure, just connection.

6. Apologize Without Shame

You're afraid to tell your kids you're sorry because you think it undermines your authority. But humility doesn't make you smaller, it makes the home safer. Children learn grace best by receiving it from you.

℞ **Scripture Dose:** *"Clothe yourselves with compassion, kindness, humility, gentleness and patience."* Colossians 3:12 (NIV)

Practical Step: Next time you lose your temper, don't just say "sorry" explain why. I was tired and frustrated, and I took it out on you. I love you, and I'll do better." That kind of honesty disarms shame.

7. Stop Measuring Their Love by Their Gratitude

You want to feel appreciated, that's human. But if you rely on their thank-you to feel valued, you'll always live disappointed. You're parenting for an audience of One.

℞ **Scripture Dose:** *"Whatever you do, work at it with all your heart, as working for the Lord, not for human masters."* Colossians 3:23 (NIV)

Practical Step: The next time you feel unseen, pray: "God, remind me that You see every unseen act of love." He keeps better records than anyone else.

8. Heal the Inner Child While Raising Yours

Some of your parenting frustration comes from wounds your parents never healed. You're reacting to echoes of your own childhood. You can't fix what you refuse to face.

℞ **Scripture Dose:** *"He heals the brokenhearted and binds up their wounds."* Psalm 147:3 (NIV)

Practical Step: Write a letter to your younger self, the one who needs grace. Then become that grace for your children.

9. Let Gratitude Reset the Atmosphere

Gratitude is the antidote to resentment. When you start thanking God for your children, even when they're loud, messy, or moody, your heart softens.

℞ **Scripture Dose:** *"Give thanks in all circumstances."* 1 Thessalonians 5:18 (NIV)

Practical Step: End every night with one sentence of gratitude: "God, thank You for _______ about my child today." Gratitude invites joy back into the house.

10. Relearn Joy Through Grace

Bitterness steals joy: grace restores it. Joy isn't a reward for perfect kids; it is the fruit of a surrendered heart. Parenting through grace turns chaos into connection and exhaustion into empathy.

℞ **Scripture Dose:** *"The joy of the Lord is your strength."* Nehemiah 8:10 (NIV)

Practical Step: Do something fun with your children this week, not out of obligation, but celebration. Joy rebuilds what guilt tore down.

Prescription Summary		
TREATMENT	**DOSAGE**	**PURPOSE**
Grace	Constant	Replaces guilt with peace
Rest	Weekly	Prevents burnout and resentment
Gratitude	Daily	Restores joy in parenting
Communication	Open	Keeps love from being assumed
Self-Forgiveness	Ongoing	Frees your heart to love again

📑 **Side Effects:** Deep breaths, softer tones, longer hugs, unexpected laughter, and peace that reminds you, you're doing better than you think.

🕊 HOLY SPIRIT CONSULT

"You're Not a Bad Parent, You're Just Tired."
I see you. I see the way you collapse into bed at night replaying every word you say, and everyone you wish you hadn't. I see the look on your face when you tell yourself, "They deserve better." I see the tears you wipe away when no one's looking, the ones you think make you weak. They don't. They make you honest.

You've been trying so hard to hold everyone together that you didn't notice you were falling apart. You're parenting on autopilot, showing up, providing, cooking, teaching, correcting, but deep down, you're empty. You love them deeply, but sometimes the love feels buried under exhaustion, guilt, and quiet resentment. You tell yourself it's normal. You tell yourself it'll pass. But I need you to know I didn't call you to survive parenthood. I called you to leave it.

You keep asking Me to fix your kids, but I'm trying to refill *you.* You want Me to change their attitudes, but I'm trying to heal your heart. I know they take and take, that's what kids do. But I designed you to receive, too. From Me. From rest. From moments that aren't filled with noise or need.

You don't need to do more; you need to breathe more. You've turned love into labor and grace into guilt. You think you're failing because you're frustrated, but frustration doesn't mean failure, it means you've been functioning on empty for too long.

You've convinced yourself that good parents never feel bitter. But even the strongest hearts can grow weary when they keep pouring without being filled. Bitterness grows where boundaries break, and yours have been broken for years. You give without pause. You forgive me without rest. You serve without space. And still, I haven't left you. I'm not ashamed of your exhaustion. I'm not shocked by your sighs. I'm standing right here, ready to refill what resentment has drained.

You've been parenting from guilt, trying to make up for your mistakes, trying to give your kids what you didn't have, trying to prove that love can fix everything. But love isn't about perfection; it's about presence. Your kids don't need the version of you that's always fixing it. They need the version of you that's still learning. They don't need your guilt; they need your grace.

I want you to stop calling rest selfish. I want you to stop apologizing for needing space. I want you to remember that you're not just their parent, you're My child, too. And I never designed My children to live burnt out, bitter, and buried under expectations they can't meet. Do you remember when they were small, how you looked at them sleeping and felt peaceful just watching them breathe? That's how I look at you. You don't have to *do* anything for Me to love you. I'm not measuring your worth by your parenting performance. I love you through it.

When you lose your patience, I'm still patient with you. When you raise your voice, I still whisper peace. When you feel unseen, I'm still watching. When you feel unappreciated, I'm still applauding. I know you feel taken for granted, but I see every unseen sacrifice. I saw the nights you stayed up when they were sick. I saw the prayers you prayed when they drifted. I saw the way you kept showing up even when your heart was heavy. You think no one notices, but heaven keeps the receipts.

You've been trying to be their hero, but that's My job. You just must be their example. You can model grace better than you can manufacture perfection. When you show them humility, they see healing. When you admit you're wrong, they see truth. When you laugh again, they see hope. Let Me carry the guilt. Let Me carry the disappointment. Let Me carry the fear that you're ruining them. You're not. You're just learning, and I use learning parents to raise world-changing children.

You can't love them well if you're resenting the life, you built around them. So, I'm asking you to come back to Me, not as a parent, but as My child. Sit with Me. Cry if you need to. Let Me refill the parts of you've been giving away. You're not disqualified by your bad days. You're not discredited by your frustration. You're not defined by your mistakes. You are seen, loved, and equipped.

Let Me turn your guilt into gratitude, your exhaustion into empathy, your resentment into renewal. Because when you're healed, they'll feel it. And one more thing, I don't just see what kind of parent you are. I see what kind of person you're becoming. You're learning grace in real time. You're discovering love beyond your limits. You're proving that even tired parents can carry holy purpose. So, breathe. Forgive yourself. Forgive them. And let Me remind you: you're doing better than you think.

📖 DECLARATIONS JOURNAL

"The Parent Trap, When Guilt Breeds Resentment"
Instructions : These declarations are meant to reset your heart and remind you that God didn't call you to perfect parenting, He called you to peaceful parenting. Read them aloud. Write beneath them. Let grace wash away guilt one sentence at a time.

💬 1. Declaration of Enoughness
I am not a bad parent for being tired. I am a human parent who loves deeply, gives freely, and sometimes needs a moment to breathe. God

doesn't expect perfection, He expects presence. Today, I release guilt for needing rest and receiving grace for being real.
Reflection: What do I need to forgive myself for as a parent?

____

____

____

____

❧ 2. Declaration of Peaceful Presence

My children need calm more than my control. I don't have to fix everything; I just must show up with love. The Holy Spirit fills the spaces where my patience runs out. I will be parent from peace, not pressure.
Reflection: What situations make me react from pressure instead of peace?

____

____

____

____

____

____

❧ 3. Declaration of Grace Over Guilt

I will stop confusing guilt with love. Guilt drains; grace restores. My parenting success isn't measured by perfection but by surrender. God is teaching me that "good enough" with Him is still holy.

Reflection: How can I invite grace into my parenting this week?

____

____

____

____

____

____

✝ 4. Declaration of Healing and Humanity

I am allowed to grow while they grow. My healing helps their hearts heal, too. Every apology I give plants humility in their spirit. Every prayer I whisper peace plants in our home.

Reflection: Where do I see myself as a parent, even in small ways?

____

____

____

____

____

____

____

💧 5. Declaration of Joyful Stewardship

These children aren't my burden, they're my blessing. They were entrusted, not assigned. I will laugh again, love freely, and with gratitude instead of resentment. Joy will return to my home, one choice of grace at a time.

Reflection: What moment with my children recently made me smile, and why did it matter?

____

____

____

____

____

🕊 **Final Note:** Parenthood is not performance; it's partnership with God. He fills where you fall short. Her parents through you, even when you feel like you've failed. So, breathe. You're not behind. You're being built.

🙏 GUIDED PRAYER

A Prayer for Parents Who Love Deeply but Feel Drained

Father, you know how much I love them, these little souls You've trusted me with. You've watched every sleepless night, every sigh behind closed doors, every whispered prayer that started with, "Lord, please help me not lose it today."

You see the parts of me that no one claps for, the emotional labor, the mental juggling, the guilt I wear like a backpack I never take off. I love my children, but I admit it, sometimes, I'm tired of being needed. I'm tired of feeling like I'm always pouring but never refilling. I'm tired of doing my best and wondering if it's still not enough. I feel guilty for even thinking that. But here I am, honest before You, because pretending hasn't healed me.

Lord, I confess that resentment has been built quietly in places I didn't want to admit. I've snapped when I meant to comfort. I've sighed when I meant to smile. I've shown up physically but I checked out emotionally. I've loved them, but sometimes from a distance, because I didn't know how to love when I was this empty.

God, I give You my guilt, the guilt that whispers I'm not doing enough, that I'm failing them, that I'm the reason they struggle. You never asked me to be their savior. You just asked me to be their steward. Remind me that You chose me for them, knowing every flaw, every frustration, every weak moment I would have. You didn't make a mistake when You made me their parent.

I release the need to be perfect. I release the pressure to get it all right. I am relieved of the fear that my mistakes will ruin them. Help me remember that You parent through me, even in my imperfection. When I feel unseen, remind me that You see. When I feel unappreciated, remind me that You reward in silence. When I feel weary, remind me that You rest with me, not after I've done everything right, but right here in the middle of my mess.

Lord, teach me to pause before reacting, to pray before correcting, to breathe before blaming. Give me wisdom when words fail and gentleness when emotions flare. Help me choose connection over control. Restore the joy I used to feel in parenting, the laughter, the wonder, the gratitude. Replace my resentment with renewal. Let me delight in their presence again, not dread the next demand. Let me see the small sacred moments I've been too tired to notice, the hugs, the laughter, the way they still look for me when they're scared.

Father, heal the version of me that's still parenting from pain. Heal the inner child who still longs to be seen. Heal the heart that gives out of guilt instead of grace. Teach me how to parent with peace, not pressure. And God, for every word I've said in anger, cover it with Your mercy. For every moment I withdrew, replace it with restoration. For every night I went to bed ashamed, reminding me that Your grace is new in the morning, even for parents like me.

I want my children to grow up in a home that smells like grace, not guilt. A home where laughter lives, where mistakes are met with mercy, and where Your presence fills every tired corner. So today, I hand You my guilt, my exhaustion, and my expectations. You can have them all. I just want Your peace. In Jesus 'name, **Amen.**

REFLECTION PAGE

"The Parent Trap, When Guilt Breeds Resentment"
Date: _______________________________

Patient Name: _______________________________

💬 **Heart Check:** When was the last time I felt joy in parenting, and what has been stealing that joy lately?

____

____

____

____

____

℞ **Spiritual Diagnosis:** Do I love my children out of grace or guilt most days?

____

____

____

____

____

Treatment Plan: What practical step can I take this week to refill my spirit and reconnect with my children from a place of peace, not pressure?

____

____

____

____

____

Faith Declaration: "God, I am not a failure for feeling tired. You are restoring my strength, healing my guilt, and renewing joy in my home."

____

____

____

____

____

____

____

Discharge Note: Grace doesn't erase the work of parenting; it makes it lighter. Rest isn't rebellion; it's recovery. You can love them better when you stop resenting yourself.

Signature: ______________________________________

Date: ______________________________________

Chapter 8:

Church Family Trauma, Ministry While Bitter

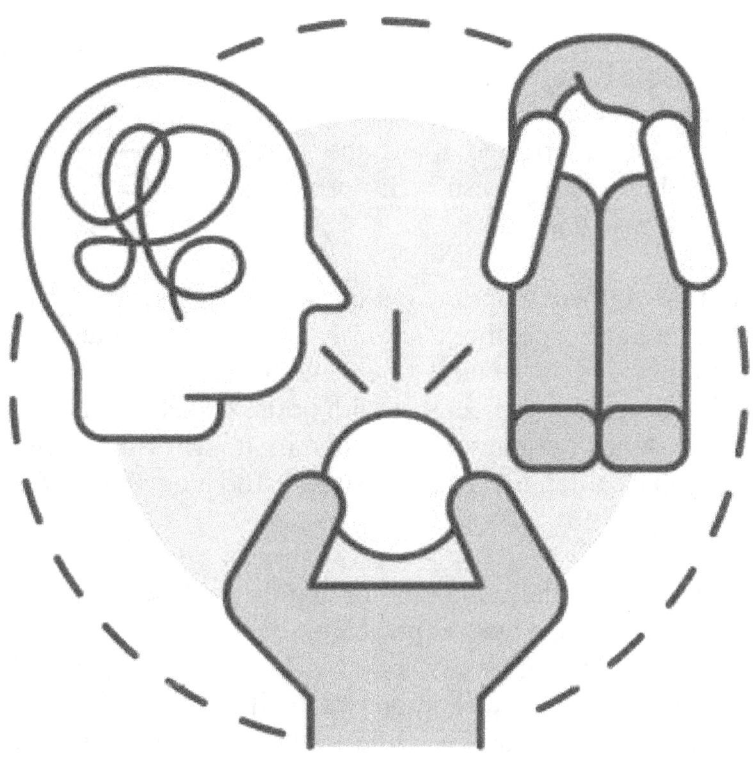

⬥ SYMPTOM: *Serving faithfully but secretly despising leadership or the flock.*

It is a strange thing to serve the same people you silently resent. You show up every Sunday, smile for the congregation, quote scripture with confidence, and pray with sincerity... but deep down, something in you is quietly rotting. You love God, but you're starting to dislike His people. You wouldn't say it out loud, but ministry feels more like managing personalities than ministering to souls.

It started small. A misunderstanding here. A betrayal there. A few dismissive comments from leadership that stung more than they should have. A group text you were mysteriously left out of. A moment when your effort went unnoticed while someone else got applause. You brushed it off the first few times, but bitterness doesn't disappear when ignored, it burrows.

Now you find yourself clapping out of obligation and serving out of survival. You keep repeating, *"I'm doing it for God,"* but if you're honest, that phrase has become a bandage for burnout. You used to serve with passion; now you serve with polite detachment. You still get the job done, but there is no joy in it. Ministry feels like performing. The altar feels like a stage. And your spirit feels... numb.

You've been hurt by the same kind of people you used to run to for prayer. You've watched leaders preach unity but practice favoritism. You've seen saints gossip like TMZ reporters and call it "discernment." You've watched spiritual gifts get weaponized for control instead of compassion. And you've smiled through it all, telling yourself that maturity means keeping quiet. But now you're bitter, professionally. You can serve, sing, lead, or intercede without feeling a thing. You know how to "turn it on." You've mastered the art of being anointed and angry at the same time. You can speak in tongues on Sunday and scroll past your pastor's message out of spite by Tuesday. You can pray for revival but secretly hope certain people don't show up.

And the worst part? You can't even talk about it. Because the moment you mention being hurt by the church, someone quotes Hebrews 13:17 at you, *"Obey your leaders and submit to their authority."* Or they remind you, *"The church is full of imperfect people."* As if that erases your pain. So, you do what most wounded servants do: you serve through the bleeding. But bleeding service leads to bitter ministry. You start losing empathy for the people you wept over. Their problems feel repetitive. Their needs feel annoying. You start dreading the same faces you used to pray over. You give advice without affection. You show up physically but check out spiritually.

You can feel it, that internal eye rolls every time leadership announces a "new initiative" or "another meeting." You used to be excited. Now, you just want to clock out. You've become cynical toward the body you were called to build.

It's not that you don't love God, you do. But you're tired of loving people who don't love well. You're tired of showing up for people who disappear when you need them. You're tired of pouring into others while no one pours into you. You're tired of giving your best to a system that sometimes feels more like competition than community.

So now, you're showing up on autopilot, doing God's work with a disconnected heart. You can lead worship while silently resenting the sound tech. You can preach about forgiveness while secretly ignoring the person sitting two rows behind you. You can coordinate ministry projects while hoping your leader fails just enough to finally appreciate you.

Bitterness turns ministry into maintenance. You stop expecting the Holy Spirit to move because you've already decided who He won't use. You start labeling people as "fake," "immature," or "ungrateful" all to protect yourself from being disappointed again. You stop letting God convict you because you're too focused on how wrong everyone else is. And you justify it because you're still serving. But service without sincerity is spiritual hypocrisy. You've mistaken activity for anointing. You've confused loyalty to the work with intimacy with the One who called you.

The truth is, you're tired, tired of church politics, tired of fake apologies, tired of being told to "pray about it" when you really need to process it. You've seen enough dysfunction to make you distrustful. And somewhere between your first "yes, Lord" and your most recent "fine, I'll do it," your heart hardened.

Now, every new leader reminds you of the one who hurt you. Every correction feels like control. Every vision meeting feels like manipulation. You nod in agreement, but deep down, you're silently thinking, *"I've seen this before."* But here's what you haven't realized yet, bitterness in ministry doesn't just block your flow; it infects the flock. A bitter spirit leading worship releases frustration, not freedom. A bitter preacher teaches judgment instead of grace. A bitter intercessor prays from pain, not power. And a bitter volunteer serves from resentment, not revelation.

You can fake fruit for a while, but eventually, the taste gives you away. God isn't exposing your bitterness to embarrass you. He's confronting it to free you. You can't pour clean water from a polluted well. And right now, your heart's water source is tainted, not by hate, but by hurt. You're bleeding where you're supposed to be blessing.

And God is saying, *"I see your service, but I miss your sincerity. I see your ministry, but I miss your heart."* He's not asking you to quit. He's asking you to heal.

☤ TEACHING

How to minister heal, not hidden, and why unresolved hurt breeds spiritual hypocrisy.

Bitterness in ministry is one of the most dangerous infections in the body of Christ, not because it's loud, but because it's quiet. It hides behind titles, routines, and "doing what's right." You can serve faithfully while being spiritually fractured. You can love the stage but avoid true surrender. And eventually, the mask gets heavy.

Jesus never called us to serve from resentment; He called us to serve from relationship. In John 21, after Peter's denial, Jesus didn't rebuke him. He restored him. He asked one question three times: *"Do you love Me?"* Not, *"Will you serve Me?"* Not, *"Will you try harder?"* But *"Do you love Me?"* Because love, not labor, is what keeps ministry pure.

When love is replaced by obligation, bitterness finds a home. You start keeping score instead of keeping faith. You start comparing instead of celebrating. You start surviving in the ministry instead of living it. Unhealed hurt turns servants into skeptics. You start questioning every motive, theirs and yours. You start seeing people as problems instead of souls. You start filtering every word through old wounds, so even encouragement sounds like manipulation. This is why unresolved pain breeds hypocrisy. You can't preach healing and hide hurt at the same time. Eventually, what's in your heart leaks into what you hand out. Bitterness seeps into sermons, songs, prayers, and decisions, until the altar becomes an emotional outlet instead of a sacred space.

But healing doesn't start with leaving ministry, it starts with letting God minister to *you*. Before you can lead again with purity, you must lay down the pride that tells you, *"I'm fine."* God's not impressed with your attendance; He's after your authenticity. When you confess your bitterness, you unclog the spiritual arteries of your calling. You make room for the Holy Spirit to flow again. Because no one ministers effectively while emotionally constipated. You can't release what you refuse to acknowledge.

Healing begins when you stop protecting your pain and start presenting it. Tell God exactly how you feel, even the ugly parts. He already knows. He can handle your disappointment with His people because He's felt it, too. Remember how Jesus wept over Jerusalem? He knew they'd reject Him, mock Him, and still, He loved them. That's the model. He didn't serve because people deserved it; He served because His heart was healed enough to handle rejection.

You can't love your congregation while resenting their inconsistency. You can't follow your pastor while secretly judging their humanity. You can't pour into others while despising the people who didn't pour into you. Healing doesn't mean pretending nothing happened. It means allowing God to purify your response so the wound no longer controls your worship.

Romans 12:9 says, *"Love must be sincere. Hate what is evil; cling to what is good."* That means you can hate what happened without hating who hurt you. You can love the church again without denying the pain it caused. Ministry while bitter is a performance; ministry while healed is power. The anointing flows best through the broken who admit it. God doesn't use perfection, He uses surrender.

So, how do you start healing? You stop equating silence with strength. You stop venting horizontally before praying vertically. You let God deal with your emotions before you hand Him your service schedule. You take a Sabbath, not just from work, but from woundedness. And most importantly, you let people be people. The same grace that saved you is available for the ones who hurt you. The same mercy that covered your flaws is big enough to cover theirs. You can't claim to serve a forgiving Savior while refusing to forgive His servants.

Healing in ministry doesn't happen overnight. It happens in layers, confession, rest, boundaries, forgiveness, and renewal. But every layer brings clarity. Every time you choose grace over grudge, the oil flows cleaner. Every time you show up healed, heaven notices.

Ministry is holy, but only when the heart behind it is whole. God doesn't need perfect workers; He needs purified vessels. He doesn't want your performance; He wants your peace.

You can preach powerful sermons and still miss the point if your spirit's polluted. But once you surrender the bitterness, your words become weighty again, your worship becomes real again, and your compassion becomes contagious again. 

When you finally let God touch the parts of you that people trampled, you'll find new joy in the same place that once broke you. And you'll realize, you weren't called to survive church trauma; you were called to heal through it.

🔖 FAITH PRESCRIPTION

"When Serving Becomes a Disguise for Suffering."
You can quote every verse about unity and still hate the sight of your leadership team. You can pour oil on others while leaking from wounds no one knows exist. That is the deception of ministry bitterness; it hides under holy activity. You're still faithful, still showing up, but faithfulness without freedom becomes bondage in a choir robe. God isn't asking you to quit the ministry. He's asking

you to quit *ministering bitterly.* He doesn't want another burnt-out worker; He wants a whole worshiper. Here's your prescription, not to fix your church, but to free your spirit.

1. Stop Using Ministry as Medication

Ministry isn't therapy when it becomes avoidance. You can't keep covering unhealed pain with new assignments. The stage can't soothe what only surrender can heal.

℞ **Scripture Dose:** *"The Lord is near to the brokenhearted and saves the crushed in spirit."* Psalm 34:18 (NIV)

Practical Step: Before every new task, pause and pray "Lord, am I serving from love or from loss?" If it's loss, stop and let Him refill you first.

2. Detox from Church Politics

Bitterness thrives in comparison to culture. The gossip, the favoritism, the invisible hierarchies, they'll drain your joy if you keep trying to climb ladders Jesus died to tear down.

℞ **Scripture Dose:** *"Do nothing out of selfish ambition or vain conceit. Rather, in humility value others above yourselves."* Philippians 2:3 (NIV)

Practical Step: Bless someone who's being praised more than you. Mean it. Watch how fast your spirit detoxes when you celebrate instead of competing.

3. Confess Without an Audience

You don't need a microphone to repent. You need a moment with God where the filters come off. Spiritual maturity doesn't mean pretending; it means confessing before bitterness turns into blindness.

℞ **Scripture Dose:** *"Search me, God, and know my heart; test me and know my anxious thoughts."* Psalm 139:23 (NIV)

Practical Step: Write a "ministry confession" not for anyone else, but for you and God. Name who hurt you, how it affected you, and what you've been avoiding. Then pray over it and destroy the paper. That's closure.

4. Separate Calling from Culture

Sometimes what hurts you is not the Church, it's church *culture*. Culture pressures you to perform; calling invites you to rest. Culture tells you to hide pain; calling tells you to heal it.

℞ **Scripture Dose:** *"Come to me, all you who are weary and burdened, and I will give you rest."* Matthew 11:28 (NIV)

Practical Step: Revisit your "why." Write out why you said yes to ministry in the first place. Let God remind you that purpose is personal, not political.

5. Forgive Leadership Without Losing Respect for Authority

Forgiveness doesn't mean blind loyalty. You can honor their position without ignoring your pain. God sees the imbalance and will handle it better than you ever could.

℞ **Scripture Dose:** *"Do not repay anyone evil for evil... Do not take revenge, my dear friends, but leave room for God's wrath."* Romans 12:17,19 (NIV)

Practical Step: Each time you remember the offense, say out loud: "God, I release them, and I release myself from needing to be right." Freedom starts with humility, not vindication.

6. Serve from Overflow, Not Obligation

Ministry is not martyrdom. You are not more spiritual because you're exhausted. You're just empty. Stop glorifying burnout as "faithfulness."

℞ **Scripture Dose:** *"But those who hope in the Lord will renew their strength."* Isaiah 40:31 (NIV)

Practical Step: Take one week off from extra volunteering. Sit in the service without a title. Let the Word wash *you*. You'll remember why you started serving in the first place.

7. Confront Without Condemning

Silence is not spiritual when it's suffocating you. Have a hard conversation but have it with humility. The goal is clarity, not chaos.

℞ **Scripture Dose:** *"If your brother or sister sins against you, go and point out their fault, just between the two of you."* Matthew 18:15 (NIV)

Practical Step: Pray first, write later, meet last. Don't process in the pulpit, process in prayer.

8. Guard Your Private Devotion

Bitterness grows in the soil of neglected devotion. You can't lead from a dry well. If your time with God has become prep time instead of presence time, you're spiritually dehydrated.

℞ **Scripture Dose:** *"But Jesus often withdrew to lonely places and prayed."* Luke 5:16 (NIV)

Practical Step: Reclaim intimacy. Read scripture with no sermon in mind. Worship with no platform in sight. Let God pastor you before you try to pastor others.

9. Relearn Compassion for the Congregation

You stopped caring because you started carrying what only God can. Compassion doesn't mean letting people drain you, it means seeing them through grace again.

℞ **Scripture Dose:** *"When he saw the crowds, he had compassion on them, because they were harassed and helpless, like sheep without a shepherd."* Matthew 9:36 (NIV)

Practical Step: Before serving each week, pray: "God, let me see them like You do, not as burdens, but as souls." That's how ministry turns from duty back into delight.

10. Rebuild Joy Before You Resume Judgment

Bitterness makes you critical. You start dissecting everyone else's worship while yours collects dust. You become the Pharisee sitting in the pew thinking, *"They're not really anointed."* But joy humbles you. Joy reminds you that grace got you here, not skill.

℞ **Scripture Dose:** *"Restore to me the joy of your salvation and grant me a willing spirit, to sustain me."* Psalm 51:12 (NIV)

Practical Step: Write down three things that still bring you joy in ministry. Revisit them every time you feel cynical. Gratitude resets your spirit faster than gossip can ruin it.

Prescription Summary

Treatment	Dosage	Purpose
Forgiveness	Daily	Frees you from emotional captivity
Rest	Weekly	Prevents spiritual burnout disguised as faithfulness
Private Devotion	Morning	Refills what ministry drains
Compassion	Ongoing	Reconnects your heart to God's people
Gratitude	Daily	Restores perspective and humility

Side Effects: Reduced cynicism, improved empathy, restored joy, renewed perspective, lighter tone, and unexpected laughter during worship again.

🕊 HOLY SPIRIT CONSULT

"You're Still Serving Me, But You Stopped Sitting With Me."
I know you love Me. I know you mean well. I know you've been showing up even when your heart has been heavy. You keep saying, *"I'm doing this for God,"* but I need you to understand something, I never asked you to do it without Me. You've been pouring from an empty pitcher for too long, child. You've been feeding others from a table you no longer sit at. You're working for a house that you stopped living in. You've been doing My work with a wounded heart, and it's wearing you down from the inside out.

I see you when you cry after meetings, when you walk to your car with that polite church smile still glued on but tears sitting behind your eyes. I see how much it hurts when they overlook you, when they dismiss your ideas, when they misjudge your motives. I see how it feels to love a body that sometimes bites back. But I need you to hear Me clearly: I never told you to carry what I died to heal. You've made your fuel their approval, and now your tank is full of resentment. You've turned ministry into a performance because it's easier to act okay than admit you're bleeding. But pretending isn't faith, it's fatigue in disguise.

You've confused endurance with numbness. You've mistaken silence for strength. You've called burnout "obedience." And still, I've stayed. I've watched you show up tired, and I've whispered, *"Rest."* I've seen you serve through offense, and I've whispered, *"Release."* I've heard you pray for revival, and I've whispered, *"Let it start with you."* You think I'm disappointed in you. I'm not. I'm just waiting for you to come back to Me, not as a minister, but as My child. The platform is not your home, My presence is. You can't heal in the same place you keep hiding.

You've been saying, *"God, change them."* And I've been saying, *"Let Me change you."* Because bitterness is not a personality trait, it is a blockage. It is the dam that's stopping the flow of what I want to do through you. You think your frustration is about leadership, about the congregation, about your position. But really, it's about the distance between your work and your worship. You've been so busy protecting your heart from people that you've started closing it off to Me. But I'm not them. I'm not the pastor who disappointed you, or the member who gossiped, or the friend who left when things got hard. I'm your Father. I don't play favorites. I don't forget effort. I don't use you and discard you.

Come to Me. Let Me sit with the part of you that's still mad at the church but too spiritual to admit it. Let Me touch the scar you keep calling "growth." Let Me refill what the politics drained. You don't need to fake forgiveness; you need to feel freedom. Stop trying to help your way out of pain. I'm not impressed with productivity; I'm after your peace. I can't anoint what you won't allow Me to clean. Your mouth says "yes, Lord," but your heart is whispering "not again." That's not rebellion, that's weariness. But child, weariness isn't the end; it's My invitation.

You've seen the hypocrisy. You've seen the gossip. You've seen leaders fail. And still, you stayed, that's strength. But you can't heal while holding every disappointment like evidence in your case against the Church. Let Me handle that. Let Me be justice while you become healed. You don't have to defend yourself. You don't have to fix them. You just must let Me fix you. You are more than your role. You are more than your title. You are more than the ministry position they take for granted. You are Mine, before the microphone, before the meeting, before the mess.

Lay it down. The resentment. The fatigue. The hidden anger you call "discernment." The bitterness you baptize as "boundaries." You don't have to make peace anymore. You can have it. I'm still here. Not because of your service, but because of My love. Let Me make you whole again, and then, you'll minister healed, not hidden.

📖 DECLARATIONS JOURNAL

"Serving Doesn't Have to Hurt This Much."

Instructions : These declarations are your emotional and spiritual rehab. Speak to them out loud. Write under each one. Let God untie what bitterness has tangled.

💬 1. Declaration of Surrender

I am not the Savior of this church. I'm a servant loved by the Savior of my soul. I don't need control to feel secure; I need Christ to feel complete. Today, I released the ministry that became my mask.

Reflection: Where have I been serving from exhaustion instead of devotion?

____

____

____

____

____

🩺 2. Declaration of Release

I forgive the leaders who hurt me, not because they earned it, but because I'm tired of bleeding internally while smiling publicly. I won't confuse ministry with martyrdom anymore. God's justice doesn't need my bitterness as fuel.

Reflection: Who do I still need to release, by name and by burden?

____

____

____

____

____

🌿 3. Declaration of Renewal

God restores joy where burnout tried to build a home. I can serve again, not from guilt, but from gratitude. I am allowed to step back when my soul needs to breathe. My call isn't canceled because I'm healing.

Reflection: What does joy in ministry look like for me again?

____

____

____

✝ 4. Declaration of Humility

I will not let pride keep me from peace. I don't need to be right to be righteous. I will confront with love, not contempt. I will serve from wholeness, not woundedness.

Reflection: Where has pride disguised itself as "discernment" in me?

____

____

____

◉ 5. Declaration of Purity

I'm not called to perform ministry; I'm called to embody it. God, cleanse my motives, renew my spirit, and purify my heart. Let my service reflect sincerity, not bitterness. Let my heart love people again, without walls.

Reflection: How can I invite the Holy Spirit to purify my motives today?

____

____

____

____

Final Note: Ministry loses meaning when the minister loses mercy. You are not failing because you're healing, you're finally serving from a clean well again.

🙏 GUIDED PRAYER

A Prayer for Ministers Who Are Tired of Pretending They're Okay
Father, you know my heart better than I do. You see the tiredness behind the smile and the hurt beneath the "I'm fine." You see the bitterness I've dressed up as boundaries and the resentment I've called "wisdom." You see how my heart still flinches when I hear certain names and how my stomach knots before certain meetings. I love You, God, I truly do. But sometimes, I don't know how to love Your people without losing myself. Sometimes, it feels like I'm pouring cracked vessels, theirs and mine. Sometimes, I wonder if anyone even notices how much it costs just to keep showing up.

Lord, I confess that I've been ministering on autopilot. I've been using activity to mask emptiness. I've been faithful in attendance but distant in affection. I've prayed from obligation instead of overflow. Forgive me for confusing performance with purpose. I give You the anger I've been hiding, the bitterness I've justified, the disappointment I've buried, the exhaustion I've normalized. I give You every name that triggers me, every wound that humbles me, and every unspoken "why" that still lingers in my chest.

Heal the parts of me that no one claps for. Heal the exhaustion behind the excellence. Heal the distrust that makes me guard my heart from the very people I'm called to love. Heal the part of me that resents the church but still refuses to walk away. God, I'm tired of pretending. I'm tired of calling numbness maturity. I'm tired of preaching hope while living on fumes. I need You to restore the wonder of serving again, not for applause, not for recognition, but for love.

Teach me to forgive without needing fairness. Teach me to rest without feeling guilty. Teach me to lead without bitterness. Teach me to stay soft in a world that keeps hardening hearts. And God, for every leader who has hurt me, I forgive them. For every member who has misunderstood me, I release them. For every wound I've inflicted out of weariness, I repent. Let grace flow like oil again. Breathe life into my calling. Bring tears back to my intercession. Bring joy back to my service. Bring fire back to my heart. I want to love the Church again, not the system, but the people. Not the program, but the presence. Not the platform, but You.

*From this moment forward, I choose to minister healed, not hidden. I choose to serve from joy, not from judgment. I choose to be Your vessel, even cracked, but clean. In Jesus 'name, **Amen.***

REFLECTION PAGE

"Church Family Trauma, Ministry While Bitter"
Date: ________________________________
Patient Name: _______________________________

🗨 **Heart Check:** Where have I been serving God while silently resenting His people?

____

____

🩺 **Spiritual Diagnosis:** What wound in ministry am I still protecting instead of presenting to God?

____

____

🌿 **Treatment Plan:** What specific boundary, rest rhythm, or honest conversation can I have this week to protect my peace and heal my heart?

____

____

____

____

💧 **Faith Declaration:** "God, purify my motives, cleanse my heart, and renew my joy. I will no longer minister bitter; I will minister healed."

🕊 **Discharge Note: The Church that hurt you isn't the only Church God is building through you. Stay soft. Stay honest. Stay His.** You can love the Church again. You can trust again.

You can serve again, whole, honest, and healed. Because ministry is not proof of strength, it is the fruit of surrender.

Signature: _______________________________

Date: _______________________________

☑ **End of Chapter 8, "Church Family Trauma, Ministry While Bitter."**

PERSONAL NOTES

____

____

____

____

____

____

____

____

____

____

Chapter 9:

"God, Why Did You Let Them Hurt Me?"

⬩ SYMPTOM: *Holding God accountable for human behavior.*

You've never said it out loud, or maybe you have, in a whisper through clenched teeth, *"God, how could You let this happen?"* You know you're not supposed to question Him, but the question lives rent-free in your chest anyway. Because if He's good, if He's loving, if He's all-powerful, then why did He stand there and watch you get crushed by people who claimed to love Him too? It's not that you stopped believing in God's existence, you just stopped trusting His involvement. You believe He's real, but distant. You believe He's powerful, but passive. You tell yourself, *"God allows everything for a reason,"* but deep down, that reason feels cruel.

You've prayed prayers that never got answers. You've been faithful in relationships that still fall apart. You've been loyal in ministries that betrayed you. You've been generous with people who took advantage of it. And while everyone else says, *"Don't get bitter, get better,"* you want to scream, *"I'm trying, but I'm bleeding!"*

The truth is, you're not just mad at them anymore, you're mad at God. Because He could have stopped it. He could have exposed them. He could have intervened. He could have warned you. He could have avenged you. But instead, He was silent. And silence feels like betrayal when you're the one hurting. You've read about His justice. You've seen Him rescue others. But when it was your turn, He didn't show up the way you expected. So now, every time you hear *"God is good,"* you nod, but your heart rolls its eyes. You show up to church, but it's different now. Worship feels mechanical. Scripture feels heavy. Prayer feels pointless. You've learned how to talk to Him politely while holding Him at a safe emotional distance. You'll still serve, but you won't risk trust again, not even with Him.

Bitterness toward God is the most dangerous kind because it hides behind reverence. You can mask it with theology and still carry it in your tone. You can say "I'm just tired" when what you really mean is "I don't understand You anymore." You can call it disappointment when it's really disillusionment. You replay the hurt like a courtroom case. *"If You're sovereign, why didn't You protect me? If You love justice, why do the wicked still prosper? If You care about me, why did You let them win?"* You don't want to backslide, you just want answers. But somewhere between the questions and the quiet, your faith got bruised. You started worshiping from memory, not intimacy. You started praising out of habit, not hunger. You started quoting verses to convince yourself, not because you believed them anymore.

You've become a spiritual skeptic with church attendance. You love God, but you don't trust Him with your heart anymore. And that's what bitterness does, it doesn't make you stop believing; it makes you stop depending. You still acknowledge Him; you just keep Him out of the parts of your life that feel too fragile.

There's something uniquely painful about being hurt by people *in God's name.* When betrayal happens outside the church, you can label it "life." But when it happens *inside* the church, it shakes your theology. How could someone who preaches forgiveness be the one who wounds you? How could someone who quotes "love your neighbor" turn around and crucify you with gossip? So now, 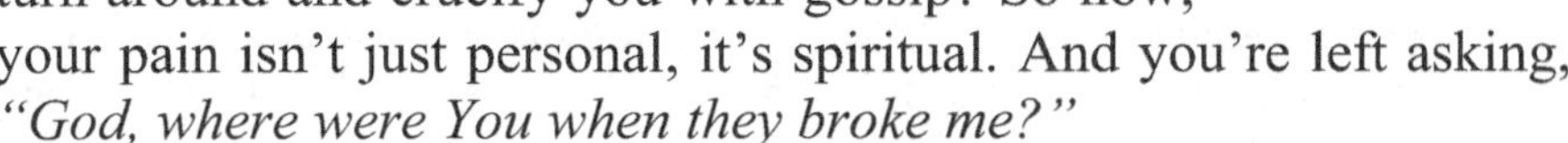 your pain isn't just personal, it's spiritual. And you're left asking, *"God, where were You when they broke me?"*

The truth? He was right there. But when you're bleeding, presence can feel like absence if you are expecting protection. You don't see the angels He sent to hold you when you almost gave up. You don't notice the strength He poured into you when you should've fallen apart. You only see what He didn't do, not what He quietly sustained. But the bitterness keeps whispering, *"He could've stopped it."* And the truth keeps answering, *"He's still using it."*

You're stuck in that tension, the ache between faith and fury. You want to believe He's good, but the wound makes you doubt His methods. You want to trust Him again, but trust feels like stepping back into a room where you once got hurt.

You've built an emotional fence around your faith, one that says, *"I'll love You, God, but don't let anyone get close again."* You call it wisdom. He calls it withdrawal. And the longer you sit in that guarded place, the heavier it gets. Because bitterness toward God turns worship into work and prayer into performance.

You're not seeking Him; you're managing Him. You treat Him like a boss who owes you an explanation instead of a Father who owes you nothing but love. But the real wound isn't just about what happened, it's about what didn't happen. You expected God to defend you. You expected Him to shield you. You expected Him to speak up. And when He didn't, it felt like He sided with your pain. Yet somehow, in the quiet, He's still calling you closer. Because what you call *betrayal,* He calls *invitation.*

℞ TEACHING

Learning divine perspective through Job's endurance and Jesus' silence. When Job's world collapsed, it wasn't the devil he questioned first, it was God. "Why?" he asked. "Why me? Why now? Why this?" His friends blamed sin. His wife blamed faith. But Job blamed silence. He couldn't reconcile a good God with the chaos he was living in. Sound familiar? That's the tension every believer faces when suffering collides with sovereignty. It's not that we stop believing in God, it's that we don't understand His version of protection. We want prevention. He gives preservation. We want to make a delivery. He gives endurance.

Job's story teaches us that pain isn't proof of punishment. It's proof of purpose we haven't yet seen. God didn't allow Job's suffering because He was cruel. He allowed it because He trusted Job's faith to withstand what others couldn't. Heaven wasn't silent because God didn't care, it was silent because God was speaking to Satan, not Job.

Sometimes the silence in your situation isn't neglected, it's negotiation. Heaven is saying, *"You can touch their circumstances, but not their calling."* Jesus modeled the same divine paradox. Betrayed, beaten, abandoned, yet silent. He could've called legions of angels to defend Him, but He didn't. Because love sometimes stays quiet when pain is speaking loudly. The cross wasn't God's absence; it was His strategy. And that's the part we miss when we're hurting, God's silence isn't the same as His absence. His restraint is proof of His control. If He doesn't stop it, He's already secured victory through it.

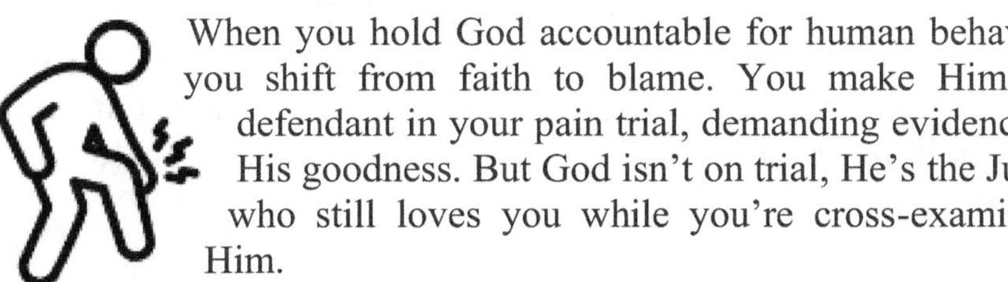

When you hold God accountable for human behavior, you shift from faith to blame. You make Him the defendant in your pain trial, demanding evidence of His goodness. But God isn't on trial, He's the Judge who still loves you while you're cross-examining Him.

Job's endurance wasn't about surviving the suffering; it was about surrendering the narrative. When Job finally stopped defending himself and started seeing God's greatness, his bitterness broke. He said, *"My ears had heard of You, but now my eyes have seen You."* (Job 42:5 NIV). That's what suffering does, it moves you from information about God to revelation of God.

You start to see that His silence was His supervision. That His delay was protection in disguise. That what others meant for evil became the soil for something sacred. Even Jesus asked, *"My God, My God, why have You forsaken Me?"* (Matthew 27:46). That wasn't doubt, that was divine empathy. He stepped into your question so He could meet you in it. You're not weak for wondering why. You're human. But the answer won't come in logic; it'll come in encounter.

God never promised to stop every hurt, but He did promise to heal every wound. Psalm 147:3 says, *"He heals the brokenhearted and binds up their wounds."* That's not a poetic metaphor, it's a promise.

Bitterness asks, *"Why me?"* Faith eventually answers, *"Because God trusted me with this lesson."* You may never get the apology you want or the clarity you crave, but if you look closely, you'll find evidence of grace, the strength that held you when logic failed, the peace that came when justice didn't, the growth that bloomed from what almost buried you.

Forgiveness starts when you realize that God's role was never to micromanage people's free will, it was to redeem what they broke. He didn't *let* them hurt you; He *limited* how much damage it could do. And if you're still standing, you're already proof that He's still good.

The same God who was silent during Job's storm spoke restoration when it was over. The same Jesus who didn't defend Himself on the cross rose three days later in victory. And the same God who let them hurt you is the same God who will heal you until you no longer need them to apologize. You can stay bitter and demand answers, or you can surrender and discover purpose. The hurt may not make sense yet, but healing doesn't require understanding, it requires trust.

When Job finally stopped asking *"Why?"* and started saying *"Though He slay me, yet will I trust Him,"* the breakthrough began. The same goes for you. When your heart says, *"God, I don't get it, but I still believe You're good,"* hell loses its grip. Because trust after trauma is worship in its purest form.

Faith Prescription

"When your 'why' finally becomes 'what now.'"
Pain tempts you to audit God's goodness. Every betrayal feels like a question mark carved into your faith. But God doesn't owe you explanations; He offers transformation. You can stay in the courtroom of *why*, or you can move into the classroom of *what now*. Here's how to start healing the wound that made you angry at heaven.

1. Let the Question Breathe
Don't choke on silence trying to sound holy. Even Jesus cried, *"Why have You forsaken me?"* Questions don't scare God; they start conversations.

Scripture Dose: *"Pour out your heart before Him; God is a refuge for us."* Psalm 62:8

Practical Step: Write your unfiltered questions to God. No censoring. Then leave space under each one for what peace might eventually answer.

2. Stop Expecting God to Be a Bodyguard
He promised presence, not insulation. Protection doesn't always mean prevention; it often means preservation.

Scripture Dose: *"When you pass through the waters, I will be with you."* Isaiah 43:2

Practical Step: Each time you replay the moment He "didn't stop," thank Him aloud for one way He *kept* you through it.

3. Read Job Without the Ending in Mind

Don't skip the restoration. Sit in the tension. Job's faith wasn't rewarded because he suffered; it was refined because he stayed.

℞ **Scripture Dose:** *"Though He slay me, yet will I trust Him."* Job 13:15

Practical Step: Spend one week reading Job 1-42 slowly. Circle every line where God speaks after silence. That's how sovereignty sounds, steady, not rushed.

4. Let Jesus Redefine Silence

At His trial, He said nothing. On the cross, He didn't retaliate. His quiet wasn't indifferent, it was restraint.

℞ **Scripture Dose:** *"He was oppressed and afflicted, yet He did not open His mouth."* Isaiah 53:7

Practical Step: The next time you feel abandoned, whisper, "You were silent, too." It will remind you of your pain, it's not alone.

5. Replace Accusation with Awe

Blame shrinks God to your pain's size. Awe enlarges Him back to His throne.

℞ **Scripture Dose:** *"Where were you when I laid the earth's foundation?"* Job 38:4

Practical Step: Step outside tonight. Look up. Pray nothing except "Thank You." Sometimes healing begins in wonder, not words.

6. Refuse to Let People Define Providence

They hurt you; God will still use you. Their behavior isn't heaven's policy.

℞ **Scripture Dose:** *"You meant evil against me, but God meant it for good."* Genesis 50:20

Practical Step: Write two columns: *What they did* and *What God is teaching me through it.* Burn the first column when you're done. Keep the second.

7. Turn Pain into Intercession

When you pray for those who hurt you, the chains start falling off both of you. Forgiveness isn't forgetting; it's forwarding the case to heaven's court.

℞ **Scripture Dose:** *"Bless those who curse you, pray for those who mistreat you."* Luke 6:28

Practical Step: Say their name in prayer until it stops feeling like poison.

8. Redefine Justice as Jesus

You keep asking God to "make it right." He already did, on a cross. Justice doesn't always mean public vindication; sometimes it's private resurrection.

℞ **Scripture Dose:** *"He will judge the world in righteousness and the peoples with equity."* Psalm 98:9

Practical Step: Each time you want revenge, visualize Christ between you and them. That image will disarm your ego faster than any sermon.

9. Let Gratitude Intercept Grief

Bitterness rewinds: gratitude reframes. What you survived didn't destroy you; it developed you.

℞ **Scripture Dose:** *"Give thanks in all circumstances."* 1 Thessalonians 5:18

Practical Step: Every night for seven days, write one thing that pain taught you about God. End each line with, "and that's enough for today."

10. Expect Restoration, Not Replays

God won't always give back what was lost, but He'll give back what was stolen: peace, joy, sleep, trust. His endings are upgrades, not repeats.

℞ **Scripture Dose:** *"After Job had prayed for his friends, the Lord restored his fortunes and gave him twice as much as he had before."* Job 42:10

Practical Step: Pray for your offenders and then list what you're ready for God to restore in you. Watch how quickly the heavens respond to humility.

Prescription Summary

Treatment	Dosage	Purpose
Honest Prayer	Daily	Turns questions into communion
Forgiveness	As needed	Detoxes heart of accusation
Gratitude	Nightly	Keeps bitterness from returning
Rest	Weekly	Rebuilding trust and resilience
Worship	Spontaneous	Replaces "why me?" with "You're still good."

📖 **Side Effects:** Tearful peace, sudden perspective, lighter breathing, laughter that feels like faith again.

When you stop holding God responsible for what people did, you'll start seeing what He's been rescuing you from all along. Pain taught you, their character; endurance will teach you His. And when you stand on the other side, still worshiping, still soft, still sane, that's the answer to *"God, why did You let them hurt me?"* Because He knew you'd survive it. And more than that, He knew you'd heal through it.

✥ HOLY SPIRIT CONSULT

"You Blamed Me for Their Free Will, But I Never Left You in the Aftermath."

I've heard every question you've whispered. Every late-night conversation where you said, "God, why didn't You stop them?" I know how many times you've tried to defend My character to your own pain. You want Me to explain why I didn't intervene, but if I showed you everything I protected you from, you'd weep harder from gratitude than you ever did from grief. You keep seeing what I am allowed to do. I keep seeing what I prevent. You think My silence was abandonment, but it was alignment. You were praying for Me to expose them; I was preparing to expand you. You asked Me to make them feel what you felt; I decided to make you stronger instead. Child, I never authored their choices, I only authored your purpose. They used free will; I used it for good. You've been angry at Me for not stopping the storm, but I was in the boat the entire time. You looked at the waves and thought I was sleeping. I was testing if you'd still trust Me when the sea was louder than My voice.

You've mistaken My patience for absence. My delay for denial. My sovereignty for silence. But I was speaking through the pain in a language your comfort couldn't understand. I was writing a future your resentment would've forfeited.

I know it hurts to watch people walk away without apology. I know it stings to see those who wronged you seem blessed. But you don't see their nights; you only see their highlight reels. Don't confuse public success with private peace. What you call unfair, I call unfinished.

You've replayed their offense a hundred times, trying to make sense of it, but what if I let it happen so you'd stop needing them more than you needed Me? You wanted them to stay; I wanted you to grow. You saw rejection. I saw redirection.

You've been asking Me "Why?" for so long that you've missed My whisper: *"Because I trusted you with this pain."* I knew your faith could handle questions without quitting. I knew your heart could endure heartbreak without hardening. I knew your story would heal others one day.

You've cried to Me about justice, and I've counted every tear. I will repay. I will restore. But before I fix what was done to you, I must free you from what's growing in you. Bitterness is not your birthright, it's a burden. I want your worship back, not your wound. So, here's what I want from you: stop demanding explanations and start accepting exchange. Give Me your confusion, and I'll give you clarity. Give Me your anger, and I'll give you anointing. Give Me your heartbreak, and I'll give you healing.

I never said they wouldn't hurt you. I said no weapon formed against you would prosper. It formed, yes, but it didn't finish you. You're still here. Still breathing. Still standing. That's proof of My protection even when you didn't see it.

Stop blaming Me for human betrayal. Stop accusing heaven of earthly failures. Stop calling My mercy neglect. You didn't see Me move because I was carrying you.

I am the God who sits beside the betrayed, the God who bled from human hands, the God who still loves while being crucified by the same hearts He came to save. I understand more than you think. So, child, let it go, not for them, but for you. Stop trying to hold Me accountable for pain I've already promised to redeem. You don't need all the answers; you just need to know I'm still well. And I am.

📖 DECLARATIONS JOURNAL

"Healing What I Accused God Of."
Instructions: These declarations will realign your perspective. Speak to them slowly. Let each one confront the lie that God abandoned you. Write beneath each statement with honesty and hope.

⊘ 1. Declaration of Release

I no longer hold God hostage to my hurt. He is not the author of my pain; He is the redeemer of it. I will not confuse His silence with His absence. He was there all along, holding what I couldn't.

Reflection: Where have I blamed God for someone else's choices?

____

____

____

____

⚕ 2. Declaration of Trust

Even when I don't understand, I will still believe He's good. Faith doesn't need full answers, it needs full surrender. If He allowed it, He'll use it. If He's quiet, He's still close.

Reflection: What situation do I need to trust God with again, fully?

____

____

____

❧ 3. Declaration of Freedom

I released my demand for closure. I don't need to know *why* to heal; I just need to know *Who*. God's justice is better than my revenge. His timing is the surgery that my soul has been avoiding.

Reflection: What closure am I still chasing that God has already completed?

____

____

____

⊞ 4. Declaration of Perspective

God didn't "let" them win; He let me survive. The pain was real, but the purpose was greater. I choose to see God's hand in what didn't destroy me.

Reflection: What hidden blessings came from what once broke me?

____

____

____

____

◉ 5. Declaration of Renewal

I will stop praying from pain and start praising from purpose. My faith no longer depends on fair outcomes, only on a faithful God. The wound was not wasted. My worship will tell the story the hurt tried to silence.

Reflection: What part of my worship needs to rise again after disappointment?

🕊 **Final Note:** The day you stop holding God responsible for people's choices is the day your healing begins. He didn't abandon you; He absorbed the impact.

🙏 GUIDED PRAYER

A Prayer for When You Don't Understand Why

Father, I've spent so much time trying to make sense of pain that refuses to explain itself. I've asked You "why" until my prayers felt like accusations. I've stared at the ceiling wondering if You were listening, or if You just watched it happen and looked away.

Today, I chose honesty over holiness. I'm hurt. I'm confused. I'm still carrying things You never asked me to hold. But I'm ready, God, ready to trade blame for belief, anger for awareness, grief for grace. You could have stopped them, but You didn't. And for a long time, I took that as proof You didn't care. But now I see, maybe You cared so much that You trusted me to walk through it and still not lose You. You were there when they lied. You were there when they left. You were there when I broke down and no one else noticed. I see now that You didn't promise to keep me from pain, You promised to keep me through it.

God, I forgive You for what I blamed You for, not because You were wrong, but because I was wounded. Heal the parts of me that twisted Your silence into abandonment. Heal the moments I stopped praying because I didn't see change. Heal the distance I created to protect myself from disappointment. You are still good. Even when I can't trace You, I can trust You. Even when I don't get it, I'll glorify You. Even when it hurts, I'll stay close.

*Thank You for not letting bitterness harden my heart beyond recognition. Thank You for carrying me through what I thought would kill me. Thank You for being constant when people were not. I give You my "why," my "when," and my "what if." And I receive Your peace, the kind that doesn't need answers to be authentic. You're still God. You're still good. And I'm still Yours. In Jesus' name, **Amen.***

REFLECTION PAGE

"God, Why Did You Let Them Hurt Me?"
Date: ______________________________
Patient Name: ______________________________

☁ **Heart Check:** What disappointment or event made me begin to distrust God's love?

____

____

____

⚕ **Spiritual Diagnosis:** Have I been blaming God for what He was trying to protect or redirect me from?

____

____

____

🌿 **Treatment Plan:** How can I rebuild trust with God, through prayer, journaling, or quiet time, this week?

◉ **Faith Declaration:** "God, I'm done holding You responsible for what hurt me. You're not my enemy; You're my evidence of survival. I trust You again."

🕊 **Discharge Note:** Pain asked, "Where was God?" Grace answered, "Right beside you." You're not abandoned. You're being rebuilt. And someday, this story will sound like healing.

Signature: _______________________________

Date: _______________________________

☑ **End of Chapter 9, "God, Why Did You Let Them Hurt Me?"**

Reflections

____

____

____

____

____

____

____

____

Chapter 10:
The Great Unlearning, Grace Over Grudges

● SYMPTOM: *Emotional fatigue from carrying years of spiritual weight.*

You can only carry resentment for so long before it starts carrying you. The irony of bitterness is that it feels like control, but really, it's captivity in disguise. You think you're holding people accountable, but you're handcuffed to memories that never clock out.

Bitterness ages you in places your face cream can't reach. You can tell when it's set in, your joy feels heavy, your smile feels rehearsed, and your peace feels conditional. You keep replaying the past like it owes you something, and every time you hit play, your soul pays the bill. You used to cry. Now you just feel tired. Not the "need a nap" tired, the kind of tired that sits in your bones, where even silence feels loud. You used to want to heal; now you just want to stop feeling. Because forgiving people who never apologized is exhausting. Letting go of what shaped your identity feels terrifying.

You've learned to function while fractured. You can pray for others and still secretly wish God would give you front-row seats to their conviction. You can talk about freedom while living emotionally imprisoned by what "should've been." You've told yourself, *"I'm over it,"* but your body disagrees, your jaw still clenches at their name, your chest still tightens at the thought of running into them, and your tone still shifts when you retell the story.

You keep saying, *"I've moved on,"* but your peace is proof you haven't. Because when you've really forgiven, the story loses its sting. But right now, every mention of their name still tastes like acid. This is what spiritual fatigue looks like. You're not weak; you're weary. You've been carrying the emotional weight of everyone else's sin against you like it's your cross to bear. You think holding grudges is justice, but its judgment disguised as righteousness.

Grudges rot the heart slowly. You start out protecting your boundaries, but eventually, you're just building walls. You stop letting people in because the ones who once did left scars where trust used to live. You stop believing in reconciliation because the last time you tried, they weaponized your vulnerability. And now, your faith feels transactional, "I'll forgive if they change." But grace doesn't negotiate. It was released. You've 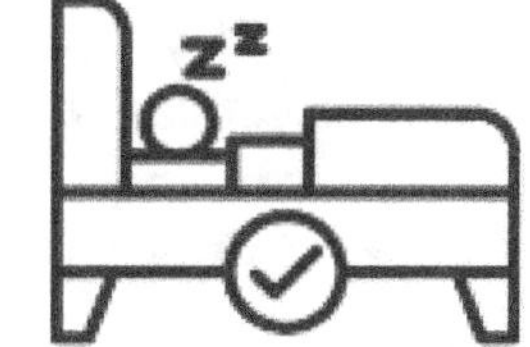 spiritualized your exhaustion by calling it "discernment," but the truth is simpler: you're tired of being hurt. You're tired of trying to understand people who never cared to understand you. You're tired of extending grace when it feels like enabling.

You're tired of feeling like the "bigger person" when no one ever seems to grow up but you. But here's the unspoken truth: forgiveness isn't for them; it's for your nervous system. You've been running on adrenaline and unhealed emotion for years. Your body doesn't know the difference between bitterness and danger; it's been in fight-or-flight mode since the betrayal. That's why your peace feels foreign, you haven't lived in it long enough to recognize it. And spiritually? You've confused survival with strength. You've built a theology that says, "I can handle it," when God's heart has been whispering, "You don't have to." You see, grace doesn't just cleanse sin, it cleanses stress.

When you withhold forgiveness, you block the flow of peace that keeps your heart steady. The Holy Spirit becomes background noise when resentment becomes your soundtrack. You've prayed for breakthrough but kept bitterness in your back pocket. You've asked God for rest but refused to drop what's been weighing you down. And every time He tries to heal the wound, you protect it like a pet.

Here's the great irony: the grudge has become your comfort. It's predictable. It gives you an identity. It tells you you're still in control. But healing demands you unlearn that pattern. You can't hold a sword and receive grace at the same time.

You've convinced yourself that forgiveness means forgetting, it doesn't. It means refusing to rehearse. You may never forget what they did, but you can stop letting it dictate who you become. And yes, forgiveness feels unfair when the pain feels unacknowledged. But unforgiveness keeps you trapped in a story God is trying to rewrite. You can't move into new peace with old pain still living rent-free.

You're not just emotionally fatigued, you're spiritually dehydrated. You've been drinking from the cup of self-protection instead of the living water of grace. And the symptoms are showing cynicism, exhaustion, irritability, and sarcasm dressed up as wisdom. You've stopped believing people can change because you've forgotten that *you* did.

You've learned to love God with your mind but not your memory. You trust Him with your future, but not your past. Because the past still hurts and letting it go feels like letting them off the hook. But grace doesn't excuse, it exposes. It reveals how much damage resentment has done to *you*.

You don't need another person to say, "I'm sorry" you need your heart to say, "I'm done." Because bitterness doesn't just live in your emotions, it rewires your spirit. It teaches you to flinch at love and freeze in vulnerability. It convinces you that mercy is weakness and that strength is silence. But that's not Kingdom living. That's trauma management in a holy disguise.

Forgiveness is the great unlearning. It's the moment you stop rehearsing pain and start remembering peace. It's not the erasure of memory; it's the editing of meaning. You rewrite the script from *"I can't believe they did that to me"* to *"Look what God did through me despite it."* And that's where your emotional healing begins, not in forgetting what broke you, but in learning to stop letting it define you.

⚕ TEACHING

How biblical forgiveness rewires your emotional system and detoxes generational pain.

Forgiveness is not emotional amnesia, it's spiritual realignment. It doesn't mean you approve of what happened; it means you refuse to live under its emotional jurisdiction any longer. Ephesians 4:31-32 says, *"Get rid of all bitterness, rage and anger... Be kind and compassionate to one another, forgiving each other, just as in Christ God forgave you."* That's not a suggestion; it's a spiritual prescription. Because unforgiveness isn't just a moral issue, it's a neurological one.

Science confirms what Scripture already revealed: holding onto grudges keeps your brain in a constant state of alert. Your stress hormones spike, your sleep suffers, and your empathy shuts down. That's why bitterness feels like exhaustion, it's emotional inflammation.

When the Bible says, *"Be transformed by the renewing of your mind"* (Romans 12:2), it's not poetic; it's physiological. Every time you choose grace, your brain rewires itself toward peace. Forgiveness detoxes your soul the same way repentance detoxes your spirit. It's divine therapy for trauma you didn't choose but can still overcome.

Jesus modeled this healing on the cross. His words, *"Father, forgive them, for they do not know what they are doing"* (Luke 23:34), weren't passive. They were powerful. He was releasing the very people who crucified Him so that death couldn't have the last word. Forgiveness wasn't weakness; it was warfare.

 Every time you forgive, you disarm the generational pattern that says, *"We don't let things go in this family."* You stop the spiritual inheritance of anger that's been quietly passed down like a cursed family heirloom.

Bitterness isn't just your story, it's often generational. Your grandmother nursed grudges. Your father avoided apologies. Your mother learned to stay strong instead of staying soft. You inherited their coping mechanisms, not their healing. But now, you get to rewrite the cycle.

Forgiveness is generational surgery. It cuts the artery of emotional toxicity that's been feeding your lineage for decades. When you forgive, you don't just heal your heart, you heal your bloodline. You cannot become the person God designed you to be while clinging to the personality pain created.

Forgiveness is the divine reset button that restores your original emotional setting: peace, not paranoia. Grace does not grudge. Love does not loop. But here's what forgiveness isn't: reconciliation without boundaries. Jesus forgave His accusers, but He didn't invite them to dinner after the resurrection. He faced them, freed them, and moved forward. You can forgive someone and still guard your peace. You can extend grace without reopening access. True forgiveness doesn't deny the wound; it acknowledges the Healer. It says, *"Yes, they hurt me, but they don't own the rest of my story."*

Grace rewires your emotional system by teaching your body how to rest again. You stop expecting pain to show up in every room. You stop bracing for betrayal in every conversation. You stop interpreting safety as boredom. Grace retrains your nervous system to recognize peace without panic. And spiritually, it realigns your theology.

Forgiveness teaches you that God's justice isn't delayed, it's divine. That vengeance belongs to Him, not you (Romans 12:19). That He doesn't need your bitterness to balance the scales; He's already settled the debt. When you forgive, you join God in His character. You start reflecting His mercy instead of mirroring their mistakes. You stop replaying trauma and start rehearsing truth.

Here's the miracle: the more you forgive, the freer you feel. The more you release, the lighter your faith becomes. You'll find yourself laughing again, sleeping again, trusting again, not because the past changed, but because your heart finally did.

Grace over grudges is not denial; it's deliverance. It's what happens when the pain that shaped you meets the grace that remakes you. And when you finally unlearn bitterness, you'll realize you never lost peace. It was just buried under everything you refused to let go of. That's the great unlearning: Trading resentment for rest. Justice for joy. The grudge for grace.

FAITH PRESCRIPTION

"Grace is God's detox plan for your emotional immune system."
When you've been hurt long enough, holding grudges starts to feel like survival. But grace is not a weakness, it's a healing strategy. God doesn't prescribe grace to make you look "nice"; He prescribes it to keep you whole. Unforgiveness is inflammation to the soul, but grace? Grace is rest in liquid form. Here's how to take your medicine:

1. Admit the Weight

You can't release what you won't acknowledge. Stop pretending you're fine. Say it out loud: "This hurt me." Honesty is heaven's first access point to healing.

℞ **Scripture Dose:** *"Cast all your anxiety on Him because He cares for you."* 1 Peter 5:7

Practical Step: Write down every person or memory that still feels heavy. Lay it physically at the foot of a cross or altar. Leave it there, no retrieval trips.

2. Trade the Role of Judge for Witness
You don't need to convict them; that's above your pay grade. Your job is to testify of God's mercy, not manage His justice.

℞ **Scripture Dose:** *"Do not take revenge… leave room for God's wrath."* Romans 12:19

Practical Step: Each time you feel the urge to "prove a point," say aloud: "God handles the courtroom; I handle the healing."

3. Choose Grace on Repeat
Forgiveness isn't an act, it's a playlist. Every time you're reminded of the offense, hit play on grace again.

℞ **Scripture Dose:** *"How often shall I forgive? Up to seventy times seven."* Matthew 18:21-22

Practical Step: Create a "Grace Journal." Every page begins with: "Today, I choose not to rehearse the hurt."

4. Guard Your Energy
Bitterness is an energy thief. Grace is an energy generator. Stop feeding conversations that drain you of peace.

℞ **Scripture Dose:** *"Above all else, guard your heart, for everything you do flows from it."* Proverbs 4:23

Practical Step: Do a "peace audit." Who or what is your calm? Set boundaries with prayer, not pettiness.

5. Reframe the Narrative

Forgiveness isn't erasing the past; it's editing how you tell it. You're not the victim; you're the evidence of victory.

℞ **Scripture Dose:** *"You intended to harm me, but God intended it for good."* Genesis 50:20

Practical Step: Rewrite your story in one sentence that ends with hope. Example: "They broke me, but God rebuilt me better."

6. Practice Emotional Sabbaths

You can't keep reliving trauma and expect peace to visit. Schedule mental rest days, where you refuse to overthink what God's already handled.

℞ **Scripture Dose:** *"Be still and know that I am God."* Psalm 46:10

Practical Step: Unplug for one hour daily, no scrolling, no venting, no rehashing. Let quietly be your counselor.

7. Replace Bitterness with Blessing

You cannot curse someone and expect to heal simultaneously. Bless them, not for their sake, but for your freedom.

℞ **Scripture Dose:** *"Bless those who curse you."* Luke 6:28

Practical Step: Pray for the person's transformation without sarcasm. Watch how quickly peace visits your house again.

8. Pass Down Peace, Not Pain

What you don't release becomes your children's emotional inheritance. End the curse where it started.

℞ **Scripture Dose:** *"The Lord bless you and keep you… and give you peace."* Numbers 6:24-26

Practical Step: Speak healing over your bloodline. Say: "Unforgiveness stops with me. Peace begins with us."

9. Let Gratitude Finish the Work

Grace begins with forgiveness; gratitude maintains it. A thankful heart is unoffendable.

℞ **Scripture Dose:** *"Give thanks in all circumstances."* 1 Thessalonians 5:18

Practical Step: End every prayer with one sentence of gratitude for what the pain taught you.

10. Remember the Cross Is Proof

Forgiveness cost heaven everything. If Jesus could say, "Father, forgive," while hanging on wood, you can say it while healing in flesh.

℞ **Scripture Dose:** *"He himself bore our sins in His body on the cross."* 1 Peter 2:24

Practical Step: Picture the cross between you and the person who hurt you. Every time the memory rises, let the cross answer instead of your mouth.

📋 **Side Effects:** Unexpected peace, lighter emotions, restored sleep, laughter at random moments, freedom from overthinking, sudden compassion for old enemies, and joy that makes no logical sense.

🕊 HOLY SPIRIT CONSULT

"You can't hold grace and a grudge at the same time."
I see how long you've carried this, child. The weight of words that never should've been said. The pressure of proving you're fine when you're not. You've tried to heal while holding evidence. You've prayed while preserving pain. But grace can't grow in clenched fists.

You've kept score, not out of spite, but survival. You wanted someone to say what they did was wrong. And I do. I saw it all.

I was there when they lied. I was there when they left. I was there when you cried on the floor and still chose worship. You don't have to convince Me it hurt; I felt it too. But now, I need you to choose: do you want vindication or freedom? Because they don't come together. If I gave you justice your way, you'd miss healing My way. My version of justice restores you; yours just rewinds the pain.

Grace isn't saying they were right. It's saying I'm enough. It's your declaration that no wound is greater than My ability to redeem it. You think grace lets them off the hook, but it hooks you back into peace.

You've been taught strength means "hold on." But in My Kingdom, strength looks like "let go." You don't have to carry history like a trophy of survival. You can lay it down and still be victorious. You've learned how to survive bitterness, now I'm teaching you how to live beyond it.

Great unlearning begins here: Stop defending your right to be angry. Start defending your right to be healed. I've seen what you endured. I've counted every tear. But I will not let the story end in exhaustion. You are the chapter of grace your family never got to write. And I'm writing freedom with your name on it.

📖 DECLARATIONS JOURNAL

"I Choose Grace Over Grudges."
Instructions: Read these aloud. Then write underneath what they stir in you, even if it's resistance. Grace begins where honesty starts.

💬 1. Declaration of Release

I released the past, not because it was painless, but because I'm tired of being a prisoner. Grace is my protest generational bitterness. I choose to live light.

✌ 2. Declaration of Healing

I will not let trauma have tenure in my emotions. God's grace is rewiring my heart to recognize peace again. Healing is my inheritance, not my struggle.

✤ 3. Declaration of Renewal

I am detoxing my soul from bitterness. Every breath I take is a reminder that peace is possible. My bloodline is shifting; the curse ends here.

✚ 4. Declaration of Strength

Forgiving doesn't make me weak. It proves I am strong enough to release what crushed me. God's grace is my evidence of victory.

◉ 5. Declaration of Freedom

I will not repeat what hurts me. I will model grace, even when they don't deserve it. The cycle breaks with me, and peace begins in my home.

Final Note: Bitterness says, "They don't deserve it." Grace says, "Neither did I, but I got it anyway."

🙏 GUIDED PRAYER

A Prayer for the Weary Soul Ready to Let Go

God, I'm tired. Tired of rehearsing hurt and reliving pain. Tired of pretending forgiveness happened when I still flinch at the thought of them. Tired of feeling righteous for being resentful. But today, I bring You what's been poisoning my peace. I bring You my grudges, my anger, my exhaustion. I bring You the bitterness I've dressed up as "boundaries." I bring You my weary heart, ready for release. You've forgiven me more than I can ever count.

So, I choose to forgive, not because it feels right, but because it's time. I forgive the ones who never said sorry. I forgive the ones who acted like it never happened. I forgive myself for staying bitter longer than I should have. Teach me to unlearn what hurts taught me, to expect peace instead of pain, to rest instead of reacting, to trust again without trembling. Let grace detox my thoughts. Let mercy retrain my memory. Let joy flood every place bitterness used to live.

*God, I release the grudge, and I receive Your grace. I don't need closure; I need communion. I don't need revenge; I need renewal. I don't need to be right; I need to be free. And I am, because of You. In Jesus' name, **Amen.***

REFLECTION PAGE

"The Great Unlearning, Grace Over Grudges"
Date: _______________________________
Patient Name: _______________________________

🗨 **Heart Check:** Where do I still feel emotionally heavy?

____

____

🩺 **Spiritual Diagnosis:** What belief about forgiveness do I need to unlearn?

____

____

🌿 **Treatment Plan:** What practical step can I take this week to live lighter, emotionally, spiritually, or relationally?

____

____

◉ **Faith Declaration:** "I choose grace over grudges. What happened to me won't keep happening *to* me. Peace is my new posture."

🕊 **Discharge Note:** Grace is not a moment, it's maintenance. Keep taking your daily dose. Bitterness can't grow in a heart God keeps washing.

Signature: ________________________________

Date: ________________________________

☑ **End of Chapter 10, "The Great Unlearning, Grace Over Grudges."**

Reflections

____

____

____

____

____

____

____

____

____

Chapter 11:

"The Silent Treatment Isn't Spiritual Warfare"

⬥ SYMPTOM: *Using distance and coldness as punishment disguised as "boundaries."*

Let's be honest, you didn't *choose* to become cold; you learned it was safer that way. Silence became your armor long before you called it "wisdom." You told yourself, *"I'm just protecting my peace,"* but deep down you know it's not peace you're protecting; it's power. Because silence feels powerful when words got you hurt. The silent treatment is bitterness in a prayer shawl. It looks mature on the outside, you call it "guarding your energy" or "letting God handle it" but on the inside, it's emotional control.

You've convinced yourself that withholding communication is "spiritual discernment." But truthfully, it's a coping mechanism that's grown spiritual vocabulary. You don't slam doors anymore, you just stop replying. You don't argue; you disappear. You don't say how you feel; you wait for the other person to figure it out while calling your withdrawal "fasting from foolishness." You've turned absence into a weapon and quiet into punishment. You tell yourself, *"If they cared, they'd reach out."* But sometimes they're confused, not careless. They can't fix what you never communicated. And while you wait for them to "discern" your pain, bitterness builds a throne in your silence.

The truth is that unspoken offense still speaks loudly, just in different tones. It shows up in passive-aggressive comments, in the way you serve half-heartedly, in the slight eyeroll during worship next to the person who once wounded you. You think no one notices, but heaven does. God hears the conversations you have in your head louder than the ones you avoid with your mouth.

The silent treatment feels holy because it's clean, no confrontation, no mess, no vulnerability. You can maintain your image while still holding onto offense. It's rebellion with good manners. You still tithe, you still post scriptures, you still pray for them… occasionally, but from a safe, silent distance.

You've mastered selective availability: present enough to seem healed, but distant enough to stay guarded. You've learned how to emotionally ghost people and call it "setting boundaries." But boundaries protect peace, not punish people. What you're doing isn't boundary; its control dressed as caution. And here's the uncomfortable truth: silence is seductive because it offers temporary comfort without requiring real healing. It lets you feel strong without making you soft. But soft isn't weak, it's Christlike.

When Jesus was betrayed, He didn't give Peter the silent treatment after denial. He didn't ghost Thomas for doubt. He didn't cut Judas off early to "preserve His peace." Even on the cross, He was speaking forgiveness. Because the absence of communication is not holiness, it's avoidance. You might not scream anymore, but your silence still kills relationships, just slower. It murders connection one ignored text at a time. It starves intimacy until misunderstanding becomes mutual. You've stopped communicating to keep the upper hand, but the only thing you're winning is isolation.

You tell yourself, *"I'm not mad anymore; I've just outgrown them."* But if your heart still flinches at the thought of them, you haven't outgrown anything, you've just gone emotionally underground. You've mistaken numbness for maturity and distance for delivery. Bitterness is sneaky, when it can't find expression through rage, it finds a home in silence. It convinces you that your restraint is righteousness, when really, it's self-preservation masquerading as sanctification. But silence doesn't heal what happened; it just hides it under spiritual language. You can't pray for reconciliation while secretly hoping they feel your absence is like punishment. That's not forgiveness; that's manipulation in a Sunday outfit.

The most dangerous part of the silent treatment is how self-righteous it feels. It gives you the illusion of control, *"I'm not lashing out, I'm being wise."* But spiritual maturity isn't just about what you stop saying, it's about what you start surrendering.

God never told you to use distance as discipline. He said to speak the truth *in love.* (**Ephesians 4:15**) Not silence in resentment. Not detachment in disguise. Love communicates; bitterness calculates. And the truth is, you're tired of pretending you're okay with the distance. You're tired of walking into church and pretending you don't notice the person two rows over that you haven't spoken to in six months. You're tired of posting verses about peace while holding grudges in your heart. You're tired of being "the bigger person" in public but the bitter one in private.

You long for reconciliation, but fear vulnerability. You want to be known, but dread being hurt again. You crave connection but justify your walls as wisdom. But here's the reality: silence may have kept you safe, but it also kept you stuck. It preserved your pride but starved your peace. You've learned how to protect yourself so well that you've become unreachable, even to God in that area. Because He won't heal what you keep hidden behind silence. You think ignoring them is protecting you from more pain, but really, it's protecting the pain from being exposed. Silence keeps you in control, but grace asks you to surrender.

It's time to unlearn the lie that distance is divine. It's not warfare, it's withdrawal. And healing starts the moment you admit that silence was never strength; it was self-defense that outlived its purpose.

⚕ **TEACHING**

Relearning emotional honesty without guilt or manipulation.
Forgiveness without communication is incomplete healing. God created language not just to speak worlds into existence, but to mend hearts that have been fractured by misunderstanding. When you stop speaking, you stop showing clarity.

Ephesians 4:29 reminds us, *"Do not let any unwholesome talk come out of your mouths, but only what is helpful for building others up."* The verse doesn't say, "Stop talking altogether." It says to refine your speech, not retire it. God's solution for conflict is conversation, not cancellation.

When Jesus confronted Peter after the resurrection, He didn't give him the cold shoulder. He gave him conversation. Three denials, three chances to restore connection. "Do you love Me?" wasn't sarcasm; it was surgery. Jesus knew the only way to heal relational failure was through vulnerable communication.

That's why bitterness thrives in silence, because silence eliminates accountability. If you refuse to talk, you can stay the hero in your version of the story. Conversation risks exposure. It forces you to face your own faults, not just theirs. But vulnerability is the bridge between offense and understanding. You can't rebuild what you won't address.

Biblical boundaries are not brick walls; they're gates that open and close with discernment. They allow healthy exchange while blocking toxicity. But the silent treatment shuts everything down, including grace. When you use silence to punish, you're not protecting your peace; you're weaponizing your pain. Proverbs 18:21 says, *"Death and life are in the power of the tongue."* Notice:

not the absence of the tongue. God gave you words as tools for peace. Silence might feel safer, but it's sterile, it produces nothing.

Jesus teaches reconciliation differently. In **Matthew 5:23-24**, He  says if you remember your brother has something against you, *"first go and be reconciled."* Not "go quiet." Go talk. Go make it right. Because grace speaks, even when the other person doesn't deserve a response.

Emotional honesty is not emotional chaos. You can speak truth without yelling. You can express hurt without hostility. You can confront with clarity and still carry compassion. That's what spiritual maturity looks like, not withdrawal, but wisdom in communication. If you've ever used silence as a form of spiritual control, remember, God doesn't model that. When Adam sinned, God didn't ignore him. He asked, *"Where are you?"* Not because He didn't know, but because He wanted Adam to know he was still worth pursuing.

That's what grace does. It pursues even after pain. It speaks life into awkward silence. It replaces avoidance with empathy.

Healing requires holy dialogue. That's why James 5:16 says, *"Confess your sins to each other and pray for each other so that you may be healed."* Confession implies communication. You can't heal from what you refuse to discuss. When you stop talking, resentment becomes your interpreter. Every silence gets misread. Every distance gets misdiagnosed. People start walking on eggshells, not out of reverence, but out of confusion. You think you're teaching them a lesson, you're teaching them to fear your quiet.

And here's the subtle danger: silence can look spiritual because it's peaceful externally. But peace is not the absence of sound, it's the presence of understanding.

God never called you to ghost His people, He called you to grace them. Grace says, *"I can speak truth without tone."* It allows you to set boundaries that clarify, not punish. When you finally open your mouth again, you'll feel the weight lift. Because bitterness loses oxygen when you start speaking life. Reconciliation won't always restore relationships, but it will always restore peace.

Real boundaries say, *"Here's how I need to communicate moving forward."* Fake ones say, *"You don't deserve my voice."* And the latter always leads to isolation, not healing. So how do you fix it? You start by repenting, not just to God, but sometimes to the person you've frozen out. A simple "I shouldn't have gone silent" has more healing power than any long explanation. Because humility melts what pride keeps frozen. You may feel justified in your silence, but God's grace calls you higher, not to win, but to witness. The silent treatment might have kept you safe, but grace will set you free. Because real spiritual warfare isn't refusing to speak, it's learning how to love again after being misunderstood.

💊 FAITH PRESCRIPTION

"Your silence isn't protection, it's interruption."
When communication dies, connection follows. Heaven can't heal what you keep hidden behind your quiet. Silence may feel holy, but isolation is the enemy's favorite hiding place. This week, your assignment isn't to say *more*, it's to say *what's true*.
Here's your divine treatment plan:

1. Diagnose Your Silence
Ask yourself: "Am I quiet because I'm peaceful or because I'm punishing?" One brings healing; the other holds hostility.

Scripture Dose: *"Let your 'Yes' be 'Yes,' and your 'No,' 'No.'*
Matthew 5:37

Practical Step: Write down the last three people you've gone silent on. Circle the ones who don't know why. Start there.

2. Call It What It Is, Control
Silence feels safer because it lets you script the story. But control isn't closure. True freedom is giving up the need to be right.

☙ **Scripture Dose:** *"Where the Spirit of the Lord is, there is freedom."* 2 Corinthians 3:17

Practical Step: When you're tempted to "ghost," ask, "Is this grace or control?"

3. Replace Avoidance with Authenticity
The goal isn't confrontation, it's communication. Speak truth with tenderness, not sarcasm.

☙ **Scripture Dose:** *"Speaking the truth in love, we will grow to become in every respect the mature body of Christ."* Ephesians 4:15

Practical Step: Schedule a "courage conversation." Don't overthink it; just start.

4. Let Prayer Break the Ice Before You Do
Prayer softens hearts that words can't reach. Don't start talking until you've started interacting.

☙ **Scripture Dose:** *"A gentle answer turns away wrath."* Proverbs 15:1

Practical Step: Before addressing anyone, pray: "Lord, give me tone before I take truth."

5. Relearn Holy Vulnerability
It's not weakness to be open, it's wisdom. Jesus spoke even while bleeding.

℞ **Scripture Dose:** *"Out of the abundance of the heart the mouth speaks."* Matthew 12:34

Practical Step: Share one real emotion a day, with God, a friend, or even your journal.

6. Forgive Out Loud
Silent forgiveness stays in theory; spoken forgiveness sets you free.

℞ **Scripture Dose:** *"If you forgive anyone's sins, their sins are forgiven."* John 20:23

Practical Step: Say it, even if they never hear it: "I forgive you, and I release you." Heaven still records it.

7. Talk to God Before You Talk About Them
Your venting is valid, but misdirected. Prayer filters offense into understanding.

℞ **Scripture Dose:** *"Pour out your heart before Him."* Psalm 62:8

Practical Step: Every time you want to send a petty text, send a prayer instead.

8. End the Performance
Your silence was your stage. Take the mask off. God prefers your mess to your manipulation.

℞ **Scripture Dose:** *"The Lord is close to the brokenhearted."* Psalm 34:18

Practical Step: Confess to God, "I've been using silence as control." That's where peace begins.

9. Turn Down the Noise of Pride
You can't hear the Holy Spirit while protecting your ego. Humility is the volume knob for heaven.

⚕ **Scripture Dose:** *"Humble yourselves, therefore, under God's mighty hand."* 1 Peter 5:6

Practical Step: If you're waiting for them to speak first, don't. Make the first move. Grace walks first.

10. Let Communication Become Communion
When you start speaking again, don't aim for agreement, aim for understanding.

⚕ **Scripture Dose:** *"Blessed are the peacemakers."* Matthew 5:9

Practical Step: Each day this week, intentionally check in with one person you've avoided. Be present again.

📄 **Side Effects:** Peaceful sleep. Softer tone. Better boundaries. Laughter returning. Emotional warmth. Relationships resurrected. A lighter spirit and deeper discernment.

🕊 HOLY SPIRIT CONSULT

"I never told you to be silent, I told you to be still."
You think ignoring them is holy, but I never asked you to ghost My people; I asked you to forgive them. You've confused peace with pride. Silence has become your sanctuary, but I can't meet you in walls I didn't build. I know they hurt you. I know words were said that left bruises only heaven could see. But child, your silence hasn't protected you, it's poisoned you slowly. Every unspoken sentence has been rotting in your heart, turning into distance between us too.

You've prayed for My presence, but you've been avoiding My process. Healing isn't neat; it's noisy. Restoration requires dialogue. Adam hid, and I called out, "Where are you?" not because I didn't know, but because I wanted him to know he was still wanted. I'm asking you the same. You don't need to be right; you need to be released.

You don't need to win the argument; you need to win back your peace. You don't need silence, you need surrender. Let Me speak into the spaces you've been avoiding. I can handle your honesty. I can handle your shaking voice, your tears, your trembling confession. Just stop pretending that withholding words is holiness. I use language to create; the enemy uses silence to destroy.

So, open your mouth again. Even if it trembles. Even if they don't respond. I'm not grading your eloquence; I'm healing your honesty. You've learned to pray quietly, but now I'm teaching you to live loudly, with grace, with truth, with peace that speaks. This isn't warfare; this is worship.

📖 DECLARATIONS JOURNAL

"My Voice Is My Victory."

1. Declaration of Release I no longer use silence as a weapon. My words will heal, not harm.

2. Declaration of Restoration God is restoring every relationship my pride has frozen.

3. Declaration of Freedom My peace doesn't come from ignoring others, it comes from obeying God.

4. Declaration of Truth I can speak without shouting, confront without condemning, love without losing myself.

5. Declaration of Grace Every word I release will carry heaven's tone. My voice is an instrument of peace.

🕊 **Final Note:** Silence builds walls. Grace builds bridges. Choose bridges.

🙏 GUIDED PRAYER

"Lord, teach me how to talk again."
Father, I've been quiet for too long. I called my distance "wisdom," but it was fear. I labeled my silence "peace," but it was pride. I built walls so no one could reach me and then wondered why I felt lonely. You made me in Your image, and You speak. Every time You create, You use words. So today, I'm ready to sound like You again.

Forgive me for using silence as punishment. Forgive me for making my distance louder than my grace. Forgive me for calling detachment discernment. I've hidden behind calm expressions and holy phrases, but my heart has been screaming.

Lord, teach me how to talk again, with love, not defense, with patience, not performance. Let my words carry healing. Let my tone mirror compassion. Let my heart remember that reconciliation begins with one conversation, not one sermon. If I've gone silent on someone I should've forgiven, bring them to mind. Give me the courage to start the hard talk. And if it's too late to speak to them, help me speak to You instead.

*Replace my avoidance with authenticity. Replace my coldness with kindness. Replace my quiet revenge with holy rest. I am not called to freeze; I am called to flow. Let grace reopen what bitterness shut down. In Jesus' name, **Amen.***

REFLECTION PAGE

"The Silent Treatment Isn't Spiritual Warfare"
Date: _______________________________
Patient Name: _________________________________

💭 **Heart Check:** Who have I gone silent on that I need to forgive?

____

____

____

____

℞ **Spiritual Diagnosis:** Was my silence protecting peace, or punishing people?

____

____

____

____

🌿 **Treatment Plan:** What conversation have I been avoiding that could start healing today?

____

____

____

____

⬤ **Faith Declaration:** "I will no longer use silence as a weapon. My voice is a vessel of peace, not punishment."

🕊 **Discharge Note:** Peace doesn't require quiet, it requires clarity. Open your mouth. Speak with grace. Heaven is listening, and healing is waiting.

Signature: _______________________________

Date: _______________________________

☑ **End of Chapter 11- "The Silent Treatment Isn't Spiritual Warfare."**

Reflections

Chapter 12:

"When Family Drama Feels Like A Full-Time Job"

◆ SYMPTOM: *Generational dysfunction disguised as "just how we are."*

Let's be honest, there's tired, and then there's *family tired.* You know that kind of exhaustion that doesn't come from work, ministry, or even life, it comes from the never-ending emotional labor of being the "healthy one" in a family that refuses to grow.

Family drama has a way of consuming you like a second career. The emotional overtime. The unpaid therapist hours. Constant crisis management. The way you can't even attend a family dinner without pre-praying for self-control because you already know who's going to test your salvation by dessert. You didn't sign up to be the mediator, but somehow, you're the one trying to keep everyone talking. You're the peacekeeper who secretly has no peace. The problem solver who can't solve her own resentment. You're the "spiritual one," which somehow translates to "the one everyone calls when they need prayer, money, or emotional cleanup." And it's exhausting. Because trying to be Christlike in a house full of chaos feels like spiritual cardio. You keep quoting, *"As for me and my house, we will serve the Lord,"* but half your house doesn't even acknowledge Him, and the other half weaponizes His name during arguments.

You've tried walking away, but guilt drags your back. You've tried speaking truth, but they twist it into judgment. You've tried setting boundaries, but they call you "distant." You've tried staying quiet, but your silence gets labeled "attitude." No matter what you do, it feels like you're the problem, and you're tired of holding everyone's emotions like it's your ministry.

Bitterness doesn't always start with betrayal, sometimes it starts with burnout. The kind comes from carrying people who won't carry themselves. You've mistaken responsibility for love, and now you're angry at the weight of expectations that were never yours to bear.

Every family has "roles" that become identities: the fixer, the silent one, the rebel, the people pleaser, the scapegoat. You learned yours early, maybe you became the caretaker because chaos needed control. Maybe you became the strong one because weakness got mocked. Maybe you became quiet because honesty always caused explosions. Whatever your role, it became armor. But here's the truth: the armor that protected you in childhood is now suffocating your adulthood. The silence, the sarcasm, the cynicism, all of it helped you survive, but now it's keeping you stuck.

Family dysfunction is one of the most spiritually confusing battles because it blurs the line between loyalty and bondage. You're told to "honor your parents," but what does that mean when your parents are the ones who won't heal? You're told to "love your siblings," but what if love keeps being mistaken for enabling?

You love them deeply, but you don't like who you become around them. You shrink. You tiptoe. You rehearse conversations in your head to avoid landmines. You smile through discomfort because peace feels safer than truth. You've built your faith around keeping the family intact, even if it keeps your heart fractured. But pretending everything's fine  doesn't make it holy, it just makes it hidden. Bitterness grows best in families because proximity breed's pressure. You can avoid an enemy, but you can't avoid your DNA.

And so, you keep showing up, exhausted but dutiful, replying to the same arguments, hearing the same excuses, biting your tongue at the same manipulative comments. You've learned to call dysfunction "normal" because normal is what you've always known. But the cost is showing. You feel the fatigue in your body, the resentment in your tone, the distance in your worship. You love Jesus, but you also low-key resent Him for making you the "mature one" who must forgive first *again.*

You've learned to spiritualize survival: "It's my cross to bear," you tell yourself, as though exhaustion is your ministry. But God never called you to be the family savior, He already sent One.

 You can love them without losing yourself. You can pray for them without playing with their rescuer. You can serve them without staying enslaved to their cycles. But first, you must admit you're tired, not just emotionally, but spiritually tired of trying to fix people who enjoy being broken. Because family drama isn't spiritual warfare, it's emotional mismanagement that's been normalized for generations. And until you stop seeing your silence as "peacekeeping," you'll keep absorbing pain that was never meant for your spirit to digest.

God never asked you to make everyone happy, He asked you to be holy. And holiness sometimes looks like walking away from toxic loyalty to protect your calling. It's not rebellion to rest. It's not dishonored to draw a line. It's not cruelty to say, *"I can't keep carrying your chaos."* That's not unloving, that's unlearning dysfunction. And once you start to unlearn it, you'll realize how much of your faith fatigue had nothing to do with the devil, and everything to do with trying to be everyone's peace instead of letting Jesus be yours.

℞ TEACHING

How to recognize the spiritual roots of family conflict and learn to love without losing your peace.

The Bible never glamorizes family dynamics, it exposes them. From Cain and Abel to Jacob and Esau, Joseph and his brothers, even Mary and Jesus' siblings, family drama is as old as humanity itself. Scripture doesn't hide the dysfunction; it redeems it. But redemption begins with awareness. You cannot cast out what you keep excusing. Some of what you're calling "attacks from the enemy" are inherited patterns that no one in your family ever confronted. You're not cursed; you're called to break the cycle.

The book of Genesis is one long case study in generational dysfunction. Abraham lied, Isaac repeated it, Jacob mastered it. Repetition without reflection becomes inheritance. And what we don't heal, we hand down.

Bitterness in families often masquerades as "tradition." We say things like, *"That's just how we are."* But just because something is familiar doesn't make it holy. Familiarity is not fruit. If it produces strife, jealousy, manipulation, or exhaustion, it's not spiritual legacy; it's spiritual residue.

Romans 12:18 says, *"If it is possible, as far as it depends on you, live at peace with everyone."* Notice that, *as far as it depends on you.* God never asked you to fix what's beyond your control. Your job is to walk in peace, not to manufacture it for others who refuse it. Sometimes the most Christlike thing you can do for your family is stop rescuing them. Jesus didn't chase every crowd. He didn't force change where hearts were closed. He modeled boundaries that still reflected love.

Forgiveness is your responsibility; reconciliation is a joint decision. You can forgive and still not re-enter chaos. You can love deeply and love from afar. Even Jesus left Nazareth when His hometown refused to believe (Mark 6:1-6). Love left, but it didn't stop loving.

Grace doesn't mean access. You're allowed to say, *"I love you, but I can't discuss this anymore."* You're allowed to silence toxicity without silencing your compassion. That's not bitterness, that's wisdom guided by discernment. And yet, grace also invites self-examination. Family drama doesn't survive on one person's dysfunction; it survives on everyone's participation. Ask yourself: Am I contributing to the cycle through enabling, silence, or gossip? Am I playing savior instead of servant? Sometimes healing your family starts with repenting your role in the drama you didn't start but helped sustain.

Jesus redefined family in **Matthew 12:50**: *"Whoever does the will of My Father in heaven is My brother and sister and mother."* In other words, blood is not the only bond; obedience is. Your spiritual family may look different than your biological one, and that's okay. You are not betraying your lineage by choosing health over history. You don't have to prove loyalty through burnout. You don't have to prove love by overextending. You don't have to prove spirituality by tolerating dysfunction. God doesn't want you to be the "strong one" who never cries. He wants you to be the healed one who finally rests.

 Let's call it what it is: family fatigue is often a symptom of misplaced saviorhood. You've been trying to carry crosses that were custom fit for others. And now your soul is sore from the weight. But Matthew 11:28 still stands: *"Come to Me, all you who are weary and burdened, and I will give you rest."* That includes rest from guilt. Rest from obligation. Rest from fixing people who don't want to change.

You can pray for your family without making their choices. You can love them without losing your identity. You can walk in forgiveness while walking away from manipulation. And maybe, just maybe, the peace you've been begging God to send to your household will finally show up when you stop trying to be its provider. Because

God doesn't need another martyr in the family, He needs a messenger. Someone who will say, *"It ends with me."* Someone who will replace bitterness with boundaries, guilt with grace, and drama with divine detachment. That's your call. That's your peace. That's your freedom.

⚕ FAITH PRESCRIPTION

"You are not the family therapist, heaven already hired One."
You were never anointed to carry every relative's emotional luggage. You've been clocking into generational chaos like it's a job you didn't apply for. The truth? Your assignment isn't to fix everyone, it's to stay healed while they find their own way to freedom. God doesn't need another exhausted rescuer; He needs a healthy intercessor. Here's your healing regimen for emotional overemployment:

1. Clock Out Spiritually
You can't work overtime in dysfunction and expect divine rest. Turn in your badge as the "responsible one."
℞ **Scripture Dose:** *"Come to Me, all you who are weary and burdened, and I will give you rest."* Matthew 11:28
Practical Step: Say this aloud: "I resign from trying to be the family savior."

2. Boundaries Are Biblical, Not Betrayal
Even Jesus withdrew from crowds to pray (Luke 5:16). Your absence doesn't equal abandonment; it's obedience to the rhythm of grace.
℞ **Scripture Dose:** *"Let your 'Yes' be yes, and your 'No,' no."* Matthew 5:37
Practical Step: Before you answer any family request, pause and pray: "Am I doing this from peace or pressure?"

3. Stop Taking Attendance in Every Conflict

You don't need to show up for every argument. Silence can be sanctified when it's Spirit-led, not guilt-driven.

℞ **Scripture Dose:** *"It is to one's glory to overlook an offense."* Proverbs 19:11

Practical Step: When drama calls, let grace answer. Sometimes your best ministry misses the meeting.

4. Pray, Don't Play Savior

God doesn't need your supervision; He wants your surrender. You intercede; you don't interfere.

℞ **Scripture Dose:** *"Be still and know that I am God."* Psalm 46:10

Practical Step: Replace worry with worship. Every time you want to control a situation, say, "God, You're hired for this one."

5. Forgive Without Family Consensus

They may never admit the damage. Forgiveness isn't a vote; it's a decision.

℞ **Scripture Dose:** *"Father, forgive them, for they do not know what they are doing."* Luke 23:34

Practical Step: Write an apology you'll never get. Then tear it up. That's closure heaven approves.

6. Don't Mistake Drama for Duty

Not every family emergency is a divine assignment. Some are distractions.

℞ **Scripture Dose:** *"Let the dead bury their own dead."* Luke 9:60

Practical Step: When guilt tries to guilt-trip you, repeat: "I'm not absent, I'm aligned."

7. Stay Soft Without Staying Stuck

Grace doesn't make you gullible. Keep your heart open, but your calendar guarded.

℞ **Scripture Dose:** *"Above all else, guard your heart."* Proverbs 4:23

Practical Step: Ask yourself weekly: "Am I helping, or am I hustling for love?"

8. Recognize Spiritual Nepotism

Sometimes loyalty to blood becomes disobedience to purpose.

☟ **Scripture Dose:** *"Whoever does the will of My Father is My brother and sister and mother."* Matthew 12:50

Practical Step: Choose health over history. Legacy starts with obedience, not approval.

9. Rest Without Guilt

You can't pour from exhaustion. Rest is warfare against generational burnout.

☟ **Scripture Dose:** *"In peace I will lie down and sleep, for You alone, Lord, make me dwell in safety."* Psalm 4:8

Practical Step: Schedule one day this week for no emotional labor. No advice. No fixing. Just breathing.

10. Let God Handle What's Above Your Pay Grade

You are not the CEO of your family's delivery. Grace is the only manager who never burns out.

☟ **Scripture Dose:** *"He who began a good work in you will carry it on to completion."* Philippians 1:6

Practical Step: Every time you feel pulled back into dysfunction, whisper: "I trust You with them."

📱 **Side Effects:** Reduced guilt. Emotional clarity. Healthier sleep. Lower drama levels. Increased joy. Freedom from codependency. Deeper rest disguised as rebellion against chaos.

🕊 HOLY SPIRIT CONSULT

"You're not their savior; you're My seed of healing."

I know how heavy it feels to love people who drain you. You've prayed for peace but picked up their problems instead. You've carried grown people's wounds like assignments, forgetting that you're My child, not their cure. You've confused compassion with captivity. I never asked you to fix what's been festering for generations. I only asked you to follow Me out of it. Your job isn't to break every pattern, it's to break agreement with it today.

You've been afraid that if you stop showing up, everything will fall apart. But what if I'm letting it fall so, they'll finally reach for Me instead of you? You keep standing in the way of consequences I'm trying to use for their conviction. Step aside, beloved. You're not abandoning them, you're allowing Me to be God again. I see how much you love them. I do too. But I love them enough to let them wrestle. I love them enough to let you rest.

You've tried to manage chaos while calling it love; I'm inviting you to model peace and call it faith. You've spent years trying to earn validation from voices that will never change their tone. Stop. Let My affirmation be enough. I've already called you approved, chosen, and free. Their silence or sarcasm doesn't cancel My stamp of worth over you. Lay it down, the guilt, the constant fixing, the pressure to keep everyone okay. You are not their glue. I am. You are not their healer. I am.

You are not the foundation. I am. So, breathe. Let's go. Be still. And trust that what feels like family separation is spiritual surgery.

I'm not asking you to stop loving them. I'm asking you to start loving them like Me, without control, without fear, without burnout. You're not quitting your family; you're quitting dysfunction. That's how peace starts spreading.

📖 DECLARATIONS JOURNAL

"I'm Not the Family Fixer, Just the Faithful One."
1. Declaration of Release

I resign from emotional management duty. God can handle what I've been holding.

2. Declaration of Rest

My worth isn't measured by how much I hold together. Rest is not rebellion, it's recovery.

3. Declaration of Boundaries

Love can have limits and still look like Jesus. Saying "no" is holy when "yes" means harm.

4. Declaration of Legacy

The cycle stops here. I'm passing down peace, not pain. My future family will inherit freedom, not fatigue.

5. Declaration of Trust

God loves my family more than I do. He can reach them while I recover.

🕊 Final Note:

You can't heal your family by losing yourself. Stay grounded in grace, it's the only inheritance worth passing down.

🙏 GUIDED PRAYER

"God, I'm tired of being the family glue."

Father, you see the pressure I've been living under, the constant need to fix, hold, explain, and forgive. You see the invisible weight I've carried for people who rarely carry me. I love them, God, but I'm tired. I confess that I've confused helping with healing. I've tried to be You in situations only You can solve. I've stepped into places that weren't mine and called it compassion. Forgive me. I release my need to manage the people I love.

Teach me to love without losing my peace. Teach me to care without controlling. Teach me to let go without feeling guilty. Help me honor my family without idolizing them. Help me bless them without breaking myself. Help me see that boundaries aren't rejected, they're restoration. And God, for the people who have hurt me under the name of family, I forgive them. I forgive their blindness, their brokenness, their manipulation, and their misunderstanding. I forgive the unmet needs that made me bitter.

*I give You the responsibility I've been carrying for everyone else's healing. You are God. I am not. And I trust You with what I can't repair. Heal my fatigue. Restore my joy. Reintroduce me to rest. And when I see my family again, let them see peace in me, not pressure. In Jesus' name, **Amen.***

REFLECTION PAGE

"When Family Drama Feels Like a Full-Time Job"
Date: _______________________________
Patient Name: _______________________________

♡ **Heart Check:** Which family patterns drain me most, and why do I keep carrying them?

____

____

____

⚕ **Spiritual Diagnosis:** Have I been confusing enabling with empathy?

____

____

____

____

____

❦ **Treatment Plan:** What boundary or conversation could help restore peace this month?

____

____

____

____

____

____

____

____

💧 **Faith Declaration:** "I am not my family's healer. I am their hope in human form, modeled after the grace that healed me first."

🕊 **Discharge Note:** You're not walking away; you're walking in wisdom. Every healthy "no" you give your family is a "yes" to the peace God promised you.

Signature: _________________________________

Date: ___________________________________

☑ **End of Chapter 12 - "When Family Drama Feels Like a Full-Time Job."**

Reflections

____

____

____

____

____

____

____

____

____

____

____

____

Chapter 13:

"Unhealed Parents Raise Wounded Children, Breaking The Cycle Before It Repeats"

There's a moment every adult child experiences, that quiet realization when you start hearing your parents' voices come out of your own mouth. You swore you wouldn't become them, but somewhere between discipline and disappointment, it happened. You started parenting from the same unhealed place you once survived.

Unhealed parents don't mean to wound; they just bleed without noticing. They carry the trauma of their childhood like a spiritual heirloom, passing it down with every unchecked emotion and unprocessed memory. They love their kids deeply, but they love filters they never learned to clean. You might recognize the symptoms: the constant need to control, because chaos once felt like home. The tendency to overprotect, because neglect once shaped your self-worth. The quick temper, because silence was once your punishment. Or maybe you shut down entirely, not because you don't care, but because care once got you crushed.

Bitterness has a way of mutating into parenthood. What we refuse to heal, we end up handing down, not through genetics, but through behavior. You may have grown up watching parents who were present in body but absent in tenderness, or maybe spiritual in public but critical in private. Their wounds became normal. And now, unknowingly, you're repeating their rhythm with different lyrics.

You discipline harshly, not because you enjoy it, but because you're terrified of raising someone who hurts you like you were hurt. You keep your kids close, not because you trust easily, but because you don't. You equate control with safety. But control is just fear dressed in responsibility.

Generational trauma doesn't always shout; sometimes it whispers. It shows up in the way you sigh when your child interrupts you. It hides in the defensiveness you feel when they express disappointment. It lingers in the guilt that creeps up when you see their sadness and realize some of it came from your tone.

You're not a bad parent; you're a broken one trying to do better with tools you never got. You love your children more than words can hold, but you're also human, and your humanity is still healing. The problem is that unhealed pain turns parenting into performance. You start raising your kids to avoid your triggers instead of meeting their needs. You measure your worth by their behavior. You start over-correcting, over-apologizing, over-analyzing. Every mistake feels like failure, every bad attitude feels like proof that you're becoming your parents.

You look at your child and see yourself, the same sensitivity, the same defiance, the same longing to be understood, and suddenly, it's not them you're frustrated with; it's the unhealed version of you still living inside. And it's exhausting. You tell yourself, *"I'm breaking the cycle,"* but breaking something that's been reinforced for generations takes more than intention, it takes introspection.

Maybe your parents never apologized, so you never learned how. Maybe they used silence as discipline, so you call withdrawal "wisdom." Maybe they demanded perfection, so you confuse grace with permissiveness. Either way, you're parenting from memory, not revelation. And somewhere deep down, you feel the bitterness forming, not just toward your parents, but toward yourself. Because you swore, you'd never repeat their mistakes, but here you are, catching glimpses of the same pain wearing your reflection.

You love your kids, but you're terrified you're transferring the very thing you prayed against. You pray for their healing while ignoring your own. You pour out what's left of you, hoping love will fill the gaps trauma left open. But love without healing becomes exhaustion. And exhaustion makes you resent the very people you're meant to nurture. Not because they did anything wrong, but because they're mirrors of what still hurts.

Unhealed parents don't need shame; they need grace to start over. Because you can't rewrite your childhood, but you can edit what your children inherit. You can't erase the pain, but you can refuse to repeat it. That's where healing begins, not by pretending your parents didn't hurt you, but by admitting their wounds didn't have to become your legacy.

You can stop the cycle. You can be the first one to raise from peace, not pressure. You can parent through grace, not guilt. But you can't do it while pretending you're fine. You must face what formed you, not to relive it, but to release it. Because until you deal with the pain that raised you, you'll keep re-parenting your wounds through the people you love most.

℞ TEACHING

Breaking generational cycles through biblical forgiveness, emotional honesty, and intentional healing.

The Bible is full of broken families, not because God endorses dysfunction, but because He redeems it. From Abraham's favoritism to David's absentee fathering to Eli's sons who abused the priesthood, Scripture shows us what happens when unhealed parents raise unprepared children. The message is clear: what we don't confront becomes what we cultivate.

In **Exodus 34:7**, God speaks of "visiting the iniquity of the fathers upon the children and the children's children to the third and fourth generation." That wasn't punishment, it was pattern. Cycles don't continue because God curses families; they continue because families copy pain. But Jesus came to interrupt that inheritance. **Galatians 3:13** says, *"Christ redeemed us from the curse by becoming a curse for us."* Translation: the generational baton can stop with you. You don't have to repeat what you remember.

Healing begins with awareness. You can't break what you won't name. You must acknowledge the emotional genetics running through your family line, anger, control, control, silence, pride, perfectionism, neglect, whatever has shaped your household. Then, you expose it to the light of truth.

Joseph did this beautifully. When his brothers betrayed him, he could have perpetuated the family pattern of revenge. Instead, he said, *"You meant evil against me, but God meant it for good."* (Genesis 50:20). He reframed the narrative. He didn't deny the pain; he redefined it through purpose. That's what healing looks like.

Forgiveness doesn't erase generational history, but it rewrites its authority. It says, "This happened, but it won't own the next generation." **Psalm 78:4–7** paints a vision for healed parenting: *"We will tell the next generation the praiseworthy deeds of the Lord... so that they should set their hope in God and not forget His works."* Notice the shift, trauma retells pain, but healing retells praise.

Breaking cycles isn't about perfect parenting; it's about honest parenting. It's okay to tell your children, "I'm learning," "I'm sorry," "I don't want to pass this on." Vulnerability doesn't weaken your authority, it humanizes it.

Your kids don't need flawless parents; they need emotionally available ones. They need to see what repentance looks like in real time. They need to witness humility at home, not just hear holiness in church. **Deuteronomy 6:6-7** says, *"Impress [God's commands] on your children. Talk about them when you sit at home and when you walk along the road."* That's not religious performance, that's relational presence. Parenting from healing means you don't just discipline behavior; you disciple hearts. If you grew up with distance, learn connection. If you grow up shouting, learn calm conversation. If you grow up manipulation, learn compassion. You can't control who raised you, but you can control what you raise.

Healing is humble work. It may mean therapy, prayer, fasting, journaling, or forgiving your parents again. It may mean sitting in rooms where you stop pretending your childhood didn't affect your adulthood. But healing is never wasted, it's how heavens train generational builders.

Bitterness says, "They ruined me." Healing says, "God's using me to rewrite the story." Even Jesus modeled parental redemption. Hanging on the cross, He looked at His mother and said, *"Woman, behold your son,"* and to John, *"Behold your mother."* (John 19:26-27). He was restoring relationship even while suffering. That's the power of grace; it reconciles even in pain.

If you want to raise healed children, you must become a healed parent first. That doesn't mean perfect, it means present, prayerful, patient. It means you pray more than you project. It means you listen more than you lecture. It means you let your scars teach them how to trust God instead of teaching them how to hide pain.

God's goal isn't to make you a "better version" of your parents, it's to make you a healed version of yourself. And healing doesn't just change your family; it changes your future lineage. Your children won't have to recover from the same wounds you have. They'll grow up seeing what love looks like when it's grounded in grace, not guilt. So, let the Holy Spirit parent you while you parent them. Let Him teach you what nurture feels like. Let Him show you that patience isn't weakness, and gentleness is not surrender. Breaking the cycle doesn't start with a family meeting, it starts with repentance. It's not about confronting your parents; it's about letting God confront the patterns inside you.

It's learning to pray: *"God, heal what raised me so I don't repeat it through those I'm raising."* Because you can't teach peace from a place of panic. You can't model grace while operating from guilt. And you can't break the cycle if you keep pretending it doesn't exist. You are not your parents' mistakes; you are their answered prayers in motion. You are the generation God trusted to finish what they couldn't start. And the fact that you're even reading this means you're already breaking the cycle.

✐ FAITH PRESCRIPTION

"You can't heal what you hide, and you can't raise what you've refused to face."
Parenting is sacred stewardship, not emotional recycling. If you want to raise healed children, you must stop parenting from the same bitterness that broke you. God doesn't want perfection; He wants participation in His healing process. Here's your prescription for breaking generational wounds before they become spiritual inheritance:

1. Identify the Family Infection
Before healing begins, you must diagnose the disease. What are the repeating patterns? Anger, silence, control, comparison, avoidance?
℞ **Scripture Dose:** *"You will know the truth, and the truth will set you free."* John 8:32

Practical Step: Write out the three biggest emotional patterns you saw growing up. Then circle which ones you've noticed in yourself. Awareness is your first act of spiritual warfare.

2. Choose Honesty Over Image
Healing doesn't happen in denial. God can't heal the mask you keep wearing for your kids. They don't need the "strong" version of you; they need the honest one.

℞ **Scripture Dose:** *"Therefore confess your sins to one another and pray for one another, that you may be healed."* James 5:16

Practical Step: Tell your children one truth about your past you've been afraid to admit. Let transparency become the teacher.

3. Stop Apologizing for Boundaries
You can't be both everyone's rescuer and your child's role model. Protect your peace, that's parenting, too.

℞ **Scripture Dose:** *"Let your 'Yes' be yes and your 'No' be no."* Matthew 5:37

Practical Step: Establish a healthy boundary this week, a bedtime for your emotions, not just your kids.

4. Model Repentance, Not Perfection
Your kids don't need a flawless parent; they need one who knows how to say, "I'm sorry."

℞ **Scripture Dose:** *"The Lord is close to the brokenhearted."* Psalm 34:18

Practical Step: When you lose your temper, don't just explain it — own it. Apologize out loud. That's how you break the pattern of pride.

5. Replace Control with Compassion
Your need to control is really your fear of repeating history. Trust that God is a better parent than you'll ever be.

℞ **Scripture Dose:** *"Cast all your anxiety on Him because He cares for you."* 1 Peter 5:7

Practical Step: When anxiety flares, pray instead of micromanaging. Say: "God, You're raising me while I'm raising them."

6. Forgive Upstream

Forgive your parents, even if they never apologized. Unforgiveness is still parenting you if you don't.

℞ **Scripture Dose:** *"Be kind and compassionate to one another, forgiving each other, just as in Christ God forgave you."* Ephesians 4:32

Practical Step: Write their names on paper. Speak forgiveness out loud. Then shred the paper, that's your generational detox.

7. Stop Overcompensating

Trying to be the "opposite" of your parents can keep you controlled by them. Heal, don't just rebel.

℞ **Scripture Dose:** *"Do not be overcome by evil but overcome evil with good."* Romans 12:21

Practical Step: Ask: "Am I parenting from peace or from pain?" Adjust accordingly.

8. Invite God into Your Triggers

The next time your child's behavior hits a nerve, pause and ask, "What part of me still needs healing?"

℞ **Scripture Dose:** *"Search me, O God, and know my heart."* Psalm 139:23

Practical Step: Journal every trigger this week and what memory it connects to. Then pray through it instead of projecting it.

9. Build a New Legacy

Healing doesn't end with you; it begins with you. Your family line is being rewritten in real time.

℞ **Scripture Dose:** *"As for me and my house, we will serve the Lord."* Joshua 24:15

Practical Step: Start a new family ritual, pray before conflict, gratitude after dinner, hugs before correction. Make a new habit.

10. Parent with Presence, Not Pressure

Children don't remember perfect rules; they remember safe hearts.

 Scripture Dose: *"Love covers over a multitude of sins."* 1 Peter 4:8

Practical Step: Put the phone down. Look them in the eyes. Listen like Jesus would, with attention, not assumption.

 Side Effects: Less guilt. Fewer generational flashbacks. More laughter. Lighter parenting moments. Healthier homes. Tender hearts. Grace that grows instead of guilt that governs.

HOLY SPIRIT CONSULT

"You are not your parents' mistake; you're My miracle in motion."

You've been carrying wounds that weren't yours to keep. You were raised by people who taught love through fear, attention through achievement, or affection through performance, and I've seen every moment you tried to love better without knowing how.

I'm not condemning you for what you didn't know. I'm healing you for what you're learning now. You've cried in silence after losing your patience. You've apologized to children who didn't understand why you snapped. You've vowed, *"I'll never be like them,"* and yet sometimes you see shadows of their habits in your reflection. I know it breaks your heart, but I'm rewriting it.

You don't need to carry the shame of your upbringing. I was there even in the rooms where love felt conditional. I protected pieces of you that trauma tried to erase. And now, I'm teaching you how to love from wholeness, not survival. Your children will know Me differently because of you. They will see prayer not as punishment but as peace. They will know discipline wrapped in gentleness. They will see faith living out in laughter, not fear. Stop disqualifying yourself from grace. The same God who redeemed your parents' generation is redeeming yours.

Healing doesn't mean pretending they were right, it means releasing your right to stay resentful. Let Me parent you while you parent them. Let Me show you what unconditional really looks like. Let Me soften your tone, lengthen your patience, and widen your compassion. You're not failing, you're healing. And your healing is preaching louder than your perfection ever could.

📖 DECLARATIONS JOURNAL

"The curse ends with me, and grace begins again."
1. Declaration of Healing
I refuse to repeat what broke me. My family line begins with wholeness from this day forward.
2. Declaration of Freedom
I honor my parents, but I do not inherit their pain. God is rewriting my legacy.
3. Declaration of Grace
My mistakes do not define me; my repentance refines me.
4. Declaration of Restoration
I am learning to parent with love, not fear, with presence, not perfection.
5. Declaration of Legacy
My children will know laughter where I once knew silence. They will inherit peace because I chose healing.
🕊 **Final Note:** You are not your upbringing's outcome; you are God's upgrade.

🙏 GUIDED PRAYER

"Father, heal the parent and the child in me."

Father, You know my story, every wound, every word, every way I was shaped by brokenness I didn't choose. You know the nights I swore I'd do better, the mornings I felt I failed, and the silent prayers I prayed after raising my voice too loud. I bring You the child in me that's still scared, still defensive, still desperate to be loved right. And I bring You the parent in me that's trying to give what I never received. Heal both, Lord. Help me forgive my parents for their humanity. Help me forgive myself for the mistakes I've made while learning to love. Let Your mercy fills the gap between my intentions and my actions.

*Teach me how to parent from grace, not guilt. Teach me how to listen before I lecture. Teach me how to love without fear of failure. When I see my parents', patterns showing up in me, let conviction, not condemnation, lead me back to You. When I feel unworthy to lead, remind me that You chose me for this family on purpose. And God, let my children see You in me, not the perfect parent, but the patient one. The humble one. The healing one. I surrender every generation behind me and everyone ahead of me to Your hands. Rewrite our story with Your mercy. In Jesus' name, **Amen.***

REFLECTION PAGE

"Unhealed Parents Raise Wounded Children, Breaking the Cycle Before It Repeats"
Date: _______________________________

Patient Name: _______________________________

💭 **Heart Check:** What childhood wound still affects how I parent or lead today?

____

____

____

🩺 **Spiritual Diagnosis:** Am I parenting from peace or from pain?

____

____

____

🌿 **Treatment Plan:** What practical step can I take to model healing to my family this week?

____

____

____

____

____

____

💧 **Faith Declaration:** "The curse ends here. My children will not recover from my silence; they will rise from my surrender."

🕊 **Discharge Note:** You can't rewrite your past, but you can stop it from becoming your child's future. Healing is hereditary, and it starts with you.

Signature: ______________________________

Date: __________________________________

☑ **End of Chapter 13 - "Unhealed Parents Raise Wounded Children, Breaking the Cycle Before It Repeats."**

Reflections

____

____

____

____

____

____

____

____

____

____

____

Chapter 14:

"Family Drama Isn't A Spiritual Gift"

SYMPTOM: *When chaos becomes comfort and conflict becomes community.*

Let's be real, some families act like conflict is a love language. If everyone's not arguing, something must be wrong. If peace shows up, somebody's itching to ruin it. You know the type, the moment you say, "We're having a calm holiday this year," a cousin you haven't heard from since Easter suddenly texts, *"So... who all gone' be there?"*

Drama has been so normalized that dysfunction feels familiar, and familiarity feels safe. Somewhere along the line, you learned to mistake for intimacy. Loud became love. Guilt became guidance. Manipulation became "how we show we care." You can spot it in the small things: the guilt trips disguised as "just checking in." The passive-aggressive comments over dinner that somehow become entire debates about "how you've changed."

The backhanded compliments like, "Must be nice to be holy now." The subtle competitiveness that hides under fake encouragement. You leave family gatherings emotionally hungover, replaying conversations like court transcripts, asking yourself, *"Was I rude or just honest?"* You try to pray it off, but even your prayers sound tired: *"God, please don't let me lose my salvation before dessert."*

The truth is, you love your family deeply, but the environment they thrive in is killing your peace. And part of you feel guilty for even admitting that. Because culture taught you that loyalty means endurance. That blood requires blind tolerance. That no matter how toxic the behavior is, family always comes first. But if family always comes first, then why is your sanity always last?

Family dramas are sneaky because they feel spiritual. You'll hear things like, *"You're the Christian one, you should forgive faster."*

Or *"Don't forget where you came from,"* as if boundaries mean betrayal. You've been manipulated with scripture and guilted with tradition. But let's make this clear, family dysfunction is not ministry, and surviving chaos is not what you're calling.

Bitterness grows in families that confuse control for care. When correction becomes criticism and affection becomes obligation, love loses its shape. You end up constantly walking on emotional eggshells, never sure who's offended this week or who's silently competing with you under the guise of support. And maybe the hardest part? You still want them to see your growth. You want to prove that you're different, not better, just healed. But no matter what you do, someone will always say, *"You think you're too good for us now."* You've become fluent in fake peace, smiling while suppressing, praying while pretending, forgiving while secretly fantasizing about changing your number. You're not cold; you're tired. Tired of explaining your peace to people addicted to chaos.

Family drama becomes a full-time spiritual distraction. It drains your energy, hijacks your emotions, and steals time you could spend building something healthy. You can't grow in grace while living in gossip. You can't focus on purpose while fighting over pettiness. And here's the truth that stings, some of the "spiritual battles" you're rebuking aren't demonic; they're domestic.

The devil doesn't need to attack your peace if your family text thread already does it daily. But the real danger isn't their drama, it's how you start to wear it. You begin matching their tone, lowering your standards, retaliating in sarcasm. You start becoming what you're trying to escape. That's how the enemy wins, not by the chaos itself, but by corrupting your character in response to it.

Family drama isn't a spiritual gift; it's a spiritual distraction. And the moment you stop mistaking it for loyalty, you'll realize peace was never abandoned; it was alignment.

℞ TEACHING

How to detox from dysfunction and reclaim your peace without losing your love.

The Bible is not silent on family drama. Cain killed Abel. Joseph's brothers sold him. Miriam gossiped about Moses. David's son Absalom tried to overthrow him. Family dysfunction is humanity's oldest subplot, and yet, God still used every broken family to birth His redemptive plan.

That means this: your family may be messy, but it's not meaningless. God can turn even generational chaos into generational change, if you stop confusing drama with duty. **Romans 12:18** says, *"If it is possible, as far as it depends on you, live at peace with everyone."* Notice it doesn't say, "Live in constant confrontation trying to fix everyone." Your responsibility ends where their repentance begins. You're not required to babysit grown dysfunction.

Jesus modeled this better than anyone. When His own family didn't believe in His calling (**John 7:5**), He didn't spend His ministry proving Himself to them, He stayed obedient to His mission. He didn't stop loving them, but He stopped arguing with unbelief. At one point, His family tried to interrupt Him while He was teaching, and His response wasn't emotional, it was defining: *"Whoever does the will of My Father is My brother and sister and mother."* (**Matthew 12:50**) Translation: Family isn't defined by shared DNA, but by shared obedience.

That's a hard truth for people raised to believe blood equals belonging. But Kingdom alignment trumps earthly attachment. You can honor your family without inheriting their patterns. Here's what freedom looks like: you stop trying to change them and start choosing peace. You stop replaying the past and start releasing it. You stop forcing conversations that end in confusion and start praying prayers that end in surrender.

Bitterness festers in families that confuse proximity with purpose. Just because someone shares your last name doesn't mean they deserve unlimited access to your peace. Boundaries don't cancel love, they clarify it.

Proverbs 26:20 says, *"Without wood, a fire goes out; without a gossip, a quarrel dies down."* That means peace doesn't always come from prayer alone, sometimes it comes from silence. Not the cold kind, but the wise kind. You don't need to respond to every provocation; you need to protect your peace like its sacred property. Sometimes the most spiritual thing you can do is say, *"I love you, but I'm not attending that argument."*

Jesus didn't chase Judas. He washed his feet, gave him bread, and still let him go. That's grace, not codependency. And maybe you've spent years trying to earn love from people who only offer it conditionally. But true love never requires performance. **1 Corinthians 13** reminds us that love is patient, kind, not easily angered, and keeps no record of wrongs. So, if "family love" constantly leaves you anxious, defensive, or drained, it's not love, its manipulation baptized in familiarity.

God isn't calling you to cut them off in anger, He's calling you to step back in wisdom. You can pray for them without sitting in the same patterns. You can forgive them without forfeiting your peace. You can honor them without harmonizing with their dysfunction.

And if guilt creeps in, remember this: even Jesus said no to family demands. Even He left Nazareth when His hometown rejected Him. He didn't stop loving them, He simply stopped losing Himself trying to be accepted. That's not pride. That's maturity. That's spiritual growth disguised as distance.

If your family sees your peace as rebellion, that says more about their chaos than you're calling. So, no, family drama is not a spiritual gift. It's a test. One that reveals whether you value being liked more than being led by the Spirit. Your assignment isn't to change your family, it's to represent Christ to them. Sometimes that looks like speaking truth; sometimes it looks like staying silent. Sometimes it means showing up with love; sometimes it means staying home in prayer. Either way, the fruit is peaceful.

Peace is the proof of your healing. You can't control how they act, but you can control whether their behavior activates your bitterness. The Holy Spirit will give you the grace to love from a distance, forgive without fanfare, and live without offense. That's the family inheritance heaven intended, grace over grudges, peace over pettiness, freedom over familiarity.

And when you finally stop managing the drama and start managing your boundaries, you'll discover the miracle: peace is not the absence of family, it's the presence of God in the middle of it.

⚕ FAITH PRESCRIPTION

"Deliverance might just look like logging out of the family group chat."
You don't need to earn your seat at a table that keeps wounding you. Peace is not rebellion. Silence is not shameful. Boundaries are not

betrayal. The Holy Spirit wants to detox you from confusion and teach you the difference between reconciliation and recurring chaos. Your treatment plan begins now:

1. Diagnose the Drama Addiction

Ask yourself: "Am I drawn to chaos because calm feels foreign?" Many of us confuse adrenaline with affection.

℞ **Scripture Dose:** *"For God is not a God of disorder but of peace."* 1 Corinthians 14:33

Practical Step: When tension rises, breathe before reacting. Say, "Peace is my pace."

2. Break the Cycle of Guilt

You can honor your family and still honor your healing. Love doesn't require you to attend every argument

℞ **Scripture Dose:** *"If it is possible, as far as it depends on you, live at peace with everyone."* Romans 12:18

Practical Step: Create a "peace phrase" you'll use to exit escalating conversations, something like, "I love you, but I won't argue about this."

3. Decline the Drama Invitation Politely

Not every battle needs your attendance. Some fires die when you stop bringing your opinion as kindling.

℞ **Scripture Dose:** *"A gentle answer turns away wrath."* Proverbs 15:1

Practical Step: When a family member tries to bait you into conflict, respond with calm truth or no response at all.

4. Protect the Peace You Prayed For

Don't sabotage what you begged God to give you.

℞ **Scripture Dose:** *"Blessed are the peacemakers, for they shall be called children of God."* Matthew 5:9

Practical Step: Designate one "no drama" zone, your home, your car, or even your prayer corner. No gossip. No venting. Only peace.

5. Unsubscribe from Emotional Entanglement

You don't owe a reaction. Their chaos isn't your calling.

℞ **Scripture Dose:** *"The Lord will fight for you; you need only to be still."* Exodus 14:14

Practical Step: Every time you're tempted to engage, whisper, "That's above my peace level."

6. Let Love Be the Loudest Response

You can out love pettiness without participating in it.

℞ **Scripture Dose:** *"Do not repay evil with evil or insult with insult, but with blessing."* 1 Peter 3:9

Practical Step: Send kindness even when you feel like sending shade.

7. Relearn the Ministry of Silence

Silence isn't always avoidance, sometimes it's anointed restraint.

℞ **Scripture Dose:** *"Even fools are thought wise if they keep silent."* Proverbs 17:28

Practical Step: Replace clapping back with quiet prayer. Watch God handle what words can't.

8. Remember: Distance Can Be Divine

You can love someone without sitting in their storm.

℞ **Scripture Dose:** *"Do two walk together unless they have agreed to do so?"* Amos 3:3

Practical Step: Practice "holy space." It's not exile; it's emotional Sabbath.

9. Forgive Daily, Not Dramatically

You don't need a stage to release what's hurting you.

℞ **Scripture Dose:** *"Bear with each other and forgive one another."* Colossians 3:13

Practical Step: Each night, whisper: "God, I release the weight of today's words."

10. Choose Freedom Over Familiarity

You can't heal in the same chaos that hurt you.

℞ **Scripture Dose:** *"It is for freedom that Christ has set us free."* Galatians 5:1

Practical Step: Take one bold action this week that puts peace first, even if no one else understands it yet.

📋 **Side Effects:** Less anxiety. Clearer boundaries. Shorter arguments. More laughter. Freedom from people-pleasing. Peace that lasts longer than the weekend.

🕊 HOLY SPIRIT CONSULT

"I didn't call you to manage their moods, I called you to mirror My peace."

Beloved, you've mistaken drama for connection for too long. You've tolerated turmoil because you feared being labeled distant. You've stayed entangled because silence made you feel guilty. But I never designed family to be a battlefield for your peace.

You've been trying to carry everyone's emotions like ministry assignments, and it's left you drained. I never asked you to fix their reactions, only to guard yourself. You are not the referee for their reconciliation. I am.

I see your heart. I know you crave harmony, but harmony without honesty is performance. I'm not asking you to pretend everything's fine; I'm asking you to trust that I'm working even when they're not. You keep trying to prove you've changed to people still addicted to who you used to be. Stop. Peace doesn't need an audience. You don't need to explain your growth to those committed to misunderstanding it.

I'm not sending you back into chaos; I'm sending you deeper into calm. Let them talk. Let them misunderstand. Let them figure out that the silence they call pride is protection. You've spent years asking Me to change them, but what if I'm using their behavior to change you, to strengthen your boundaries, deepen your discernment, and teach you how to love without losing yourself?

I am healing you from needing validation where you only need vision. I am restoring your peace not through reunion, but through revelation: that peace is your inheritance, not your privilege. Stop treating family drama like ministry, it's not your pulpit, it's your test. You pass it by staying soft, staying steady, staying surrendered. You don't fight chaos with confrontation; you fight it by refusing to play the game. Peace isn't passive. It's powerful. And you're about to feel what it's like to live drama-free, not because the world has changed, but because you did.

📖 DECLARATIONS JOURNAL

"My peace is not up for family negotiation."

1. Declaration of Freedom
I am not addicted to chaos. I choose calm even when conflict calls my name.
2. Declaration of Identity
I am a peacemaker, not a peacekeeper. My boundaries are blessed, not bitter.
3. Declaration of Authority
I will not let family dysfunction dictate my destiny. God's voice outranks generational noise.
4. Declaration of Wisdom
I can love them from afar and still look like Jesus up closely.
5. Declaration of Peace
My silence is not pride, it's protection. My stillness is not weakness, it's strength.
🫰 **Final Note:** Drama doesn't deserve your energy. Save it for your purpose.

🙏 GUIDED PRAYER

"Lord, teach me to value peace over performance."
Father, you know my family. You know the stories, the secrets, the patterns, the pressure. You've seen every argument that turned into a prayer request, every silent tension that never got healed. You know how hard I've tried to love through chaos; how many times I've swallowed my truth just to keep the peace. Today, I surrender my need to fix what only You can redeem. I lay down the guilt that tells me I'm unloving when I'm simply protecting my peace. I refuse to believe that family dysfunction is my destiny. Heal the triggers that make me react instead of responding. Heal the fear that makes me perform instead of being present. Heal the need for approval that keeps me bound to people who confuse manipulation with love. Teach me to walk in wisdom, to speak when led, to stay silent when needed, and to set boundaries without bitterness. Teach me that walking away sometimes honors You more than staying and arguing.

Teach me to love them without losing myself. I choose peace. Not the kind that comes from avoidance, but the kind that comes from alignment. I choose joy that isn't based on how they act but on who You are. And when I see the same drama rise again, let me remember peace is not weakness, it's warfare. In Jesus' name, **Amen.**

REFLECTION PAGE

"Family Drama Isn't a Spiritual Gift"
Date: _______________________________
Patient Name: _________________________________
💭 **Heart Check:** What type of family chaos am I most tempted to engage in?

____

____

____

____

____

Spiritual Diagnosis: Have I been confusing loyalty with bondage?

____

____

____

Treatment Plan: What boundaries do I need to reinforce to protect my peace this season?

____

____

____

Faith Declaration: "I am not the manager of anyone else's emotions. Peace is not rebellion. Boundaries are not betrayal. And family drama is not my ministry."

Discharge Note: Peace isn't the absence of family; it's the presence of maturity. You're free to love them, but you're not required to live in their chaos.

Signature: _____________________________

Date: _____________________________

☑ **End of Chapter 14 - "Family Drama Isn't a Spiritual Gift."**

Final reminder: You were never called to inherit the family's drama, only its potential for healing. Peace is the new bloodline.

📖 FAITH CLINIC DISCHARGE SUMMARY PAGE

Patient Name: _______________________________

Date of Discharge: ___________________________

Attending Physician: **The Great Physician — Jesus Christ**

Diagnosis: **Chronic Bitterness Syndrome (Triggered by Unforgiveness, Unhealed Family Wounds, and Spiritual Fatigue)**

Treatment Administered: **Grace, Repentance, Forgiveness, Prayer Therapy, Boundary Setting, Emotional Honesty, and Faith Restoratives.**

📋 WEEKLY RECOVERY TRACKER

Monitor your emotional and spiritual vitals daily. Healing is progressive, not instant.

Week	Focus Area	Heart Vital Signs	Peace Level (1–10)	Notes/Triggers

Week 1	Identifying bitterness roots	☑ Honest reflection ☑ Journaling pain ☑ Confession w/o shame	______	______ ______ ______ __
Week 2	Practicing forgiveness	☑ Daily declarations ☑ Prayer over offenders ☑ Emotional release	______	______ ______ ______
Week 3	Strengthening boundaries	☑ "No" without guilt ☑ Time away from toxic cycles ☑ Rest as worship	______	______ ______ ______ ____
Week 4	Rebuilding peace & presence	☑ Gratitude journaling ☑ Worship instead of worry ☑ Restoring laughter	______	______ ______ ______ __

⚕ Weekly Check-In Reminder:

- Take your *Faith Prescription* daily (read at least one declaration each morning).
- Hydrate with *Scripture doses*, minimum two verses of peace or forgiveness per day.
- Report relapses to your "Accountability Physician" (a trusted spiritual friend, mentor, or counselor).

📅 30-DAY RECOVERY & MAINTENANCE PLAN

Healing is a process. The goal isn't perfection, it's progression.

Days 1-7: Detox & Diagnosis
- Acknowledge hidden anger and emotional fatigue.

- Write one prayer of forgiveness per day (even if it's messy).
- Fast from gossip, comparison, or rehashing old wounds.
- Scripture Focus: *Psalm 51, "Create in me a clean heart."*

Days 8-14: The Forgiveness Rehab
- Revisit each chapter of this edition for self-reflection.
- Call or write one "closure" letter, not to send, but to release
- Replace sarcasm with sincerity; replace shade with silence.
- Scripture Focus: *Ephesians 4:31–32 "Get rid of all bitterness…"*

Days 15-21: Rebuilding Boundaries & Balance
- Revaluate access levels, who drains vs. who strengthen.
- Spend one day offline for spiritual reset.
- Journal what peace feels like in your body (less tension, calmer tone).
- Scripture Focus: *Proverbs 4:23, "Guard your heart."*

Days 22-30: The Peace Preservation Protocol
- Daily gratitude list (3 things minimum).
- Replace worry time with worship time.
- Celebrate small wins, one act of emotional maturity = victory.
- Scripture Focus: *Philippians 4:7, "The peace of God will guard your heart and mind.*

✐ Progress Indicator:

☑ Reduced triggers
☑ Quicker forgiveness response
☑ Emotional calmness in former chaos
☑ Increased laughter, lowered defensiveness

🚨 EMERGENCY INSTRUCTIONS

In case of sudden emotional relapse, spiritual panic, or bitterness flare-ups, follow this Faith Code.

BITTERNESS CODE BLUE PROTOCOL

1. **Pause Before Reacting**
   - Take three deep breaths. Silence is CPR for your peace.
   - Don't text, call, or post anything until calm returns.

2. **Locate the Trigger, Not the Target**
   - Ask: "What wound did this poke?" not "Who's at fault?"
   - Treat the cause, not the comment.

3. **Administer Immediate Forgiveness Therapy**
   - Whisper out loud: "God, I release this moment before it becomes a memory."
   - Visualize placing the situation at the foot of the cross.

4. **Take 2 Grace Pills & 1 Psalm**
   - *Grace Pill 1:* "I am still growing."
   - *Grace Pill 2:* "They're still human."
   - *Psalm:* Read Psalm 37 or 91 until your pulse slows.

5. **Call for Backup**
   - Contact your Accountability Partner, Pastor, or Counselor.
   - Tell them you need prayer, not pity.

6. **Return to Spiritual Breathing**
   - Inhale: *Peace be still.*
   - Exhale: *I forgive again.*

🩺 **If symptoms persist longer than 48 hours:**

- Revisit your *Faith Clinic Journal* and repeat the prayer in Chapter 6 ("Forgiving People Who Don't Even Feel Bad").
- Schedule an emergency appointment with The Holy Spirit, He's always on call.

DISCHARGE SUMMARY NOTES

Final Assessment:
- Patient shows signs of emotional stabilization and reduced spiritual inflammation.
- Peace levels are increasing; reactivity decreasing.
- Forgiveness flow returning to normal rhythm.
- Bitter antibodies develop through daily gratitude.

Physician's Recommendation:
- Continue taking *Faith Prescriptions* (Scripture, Worship, Reflection)
- Avoid exposure to toxic environments that trigger spiritual regression.
- Attend regular checkups (weekly prayer, community accountability).

Next Appointment: *Every morning in prayer. The Doctor is in.*

PATIENT SIGNATURE:___________

PHYSICIAN

(HOLYSPIRIT)SIGNATURE:_______________

DISCHARGE BLESSING: "You are released from guilt, not grace. Go in peace, stay healed, and remember, drama is not your destiny."

DR. PATRICIA S. TANNER

PERSONAL NOTES

Epilogue:

THE FINAL RELEASE: YOU CAN'T HEAL WHAT YOU KEEP HATING

Congratulations. You made it to the end of your discharge papers. You've cried, confessed, forgiven, deleted some phone numbers, prayed through imaginary arguments, and maybe even threw a few invisible punches in your car while whispering, "Jesus, fix it before I do." But here you are, still standing, still soft, still healing.

Bitterness tried to convince you it was protection, but really, it was just poison wearing a halo. It promised safety, but it delivered isolation. It told you that forgiveness made you weak, when truthfully, it's what made you dangerous, because the moment you forgave, you broke a generational contract that hell had on your heart.

You thought this journey was about them. Their apology. Their change. Their growth. But somewhere along the way, you realized God never scheduled their healing, He scheduled yours. You came to the Faith Clinic thinking, *"Dear God, fix them."* And God smiled, handed you a mirror, and said, *"Let's start with you."*

Bitterness was never your personality; it was your pain's security system. It made sure no one got too close again, not even God sometimes. But healing is what happens when you turn that alarm off and let Him touch the places you swore were off limits. The scar doesn't disappear, but it stops bleeding. Now you understand that peace isn't a vibe, it's warfare. Forgiveness isn't forgetting, it's freedom.

And grace? Grace is the divine anesthesia that let God perform open-heart surgery while you were still arguing with Him about the procedure. You may not get every apology. You may not see every wrong made right. Some people will keep pretending they didn't hurt you. That's okay, they're not the author of your recovery; God is. So let this be your final discharge note: You are not your pain's representative. You are not your family's fixer. You are not the sum of your wounds; you are the evidence that healing works. You have officially been released from spiritual codependency. You are no longer the unpaid therapist of everyone else's dysfunction. You have been promoted to *Patient-Healed-turned-Healer.* You're walking out of this clinic with new language, new boundaries, new peace. And no, you don't need to explain that peace to anyone who's still committed to chaos.

You've learned that forgiveness isn't a weakness, it's holy rebellion. It's you telling your trauma, *"You don't run me anymore."* It's looking your history in the face and saying, *"You happened, but you're not happening again."*

Maybe you were raised in chaos. Maybe your parents didn't know how to love without control. Maybe you grew up thinking peace was just the quiet between arguments. But now? Now you know peace isn't the absence of noise, it's the presence of God. And that presence lives in you. Right there, in the same heart that once housed bitterness, a new garden is growing. Forgiveness has made room for joy. Grace has built new walls of protection that no gossip can breach. You've become proof that God really does make all things new, even family cycles, even broken trust, even the offended heart that swore it was done trying.

You're healed enough now to love again. To laugh again. To go to family gatherings without losing your faith. You might still feel the twinge when someone brings up your past, but that's just the scar saying, *"We survived this."*

You'll still have moments where bitterness knocks on the door, especially when you're reminded of what you lost. But this time, you won't answer. You'll smile, sip your peace, and remember you've been discharged. You are free to live without the  weight of offense. You are free to stop keeping score. You are free to forgive even if it still hurts a little, because forgiveness isn't about feelings; it's about faith. And when the enemy whispers, *"You're too soft now,"* you'll whisper back, *"No, I'm healed now."*

Healing is the loudest revenge you'll ever get. Peace is the proof you won. Love is the legacy you'll leave behind. So go ahead and walk out of this clinic, not like a patient, but like a testimony. Someone's delivery depends on your willingness to stay healed. Someone's breakthrough will start because you refused to stay bitter. Someone's family will change because you chose grace over grudges.

Your discharge summary isn't the end, it's the evidence. You survived the heartbreak. You outgrew the offense. You graduated from the Gospel of the Offended to the Gospel of the Redeemed. Now go live like you've been released. You are cleared for peace. You are cleared for purpose. You are cleared of joy.

Faith Clinic Diagnosis: Bitterness, resolved.
Treatment Completed: Grace, ongoing.
Status: Spiritually stable. Emotionally improving. Eternally free. And if anyone asks you how you healed, tell them the truth, *"Dear God, it was never them… it was me."*

📖 FAITH CLINIC SEAL OF RELEASE

Official Closing Page, Bitterness Edition

Book Title: *Dear God, It's Not Me, It's Them, The Gospel According to the Offended*

Series: *The Faith Clinic Series*

Author: Patricia Tanner

Attending Physician: The Great Physician, Jesus Christ

Case Number: FC-BITTER-001

✉ FINAL DIAGNOSIS:

Bitterness due to prolonged emotional infection caused by unresolved family trauma, unspoken offense, and unhealed expectations.
Condition: Once terminal, now treatable by grace.
Prognosis: Full recovery with continued surrender.

🕊 TREATMENT SUMMARY:

The patient underwent multiple rounds of:

- **Forgiveness Therapy:** Daily repentance and emotional detox.
- **Heart Surgery:** Removal of hidden resentment under divine anesthesia.
- **Boundary Reconstruction:** Spiritual sutures secured by truth and wisdom.
- **Faith Infusion:** Grace administered intravenously through Scripture.

- **Worship Rehabilitation:** Reintroducing peace through praise.

Response to Treatment: Positive.

Side Effects: Unexpected laughter, deep peace, healthy detachment, sudden joy, lower tolerance for gossip, uncontrollable gratitude, and random bursts of worship in traffic.

⊞ SEAL OF RELEASE

"Whom the Son sets free is free indeed." **John 8:36** This certifies that the patient has been discharged from the care of bitterness and officially released into lifelong maintenance of peace, grace, and divine maturity.

Restrictions:
- Avoid exposure to toxic conversations, emotional blackmail, or spiritual manipulation.
- Refrain from resuscitating dead arguments.
- Maintain a daily dosage of Scripture, worship, rest, and laughter.

Approved Activities:
- ☑ Loving without over-functioning
- ☑ Speaking truth in love
- ☑ Protecting peace like a prescription
- ☑ Building healthy legacy for future generations

⊙ POST-CARE INSTRUCTIONS

1. **Follow-up Appointments:** Every morning in prayer.
2. **Maintenance Medication:** Forgiveness (unlimited refills).
3. **Diet:** Consume gratitude daily; fast from comparison.
4. **Exercise:** Stretch your faith through service and humility.

5. **Support Group:** The Kingdom Family, forever open, always growing.

PHYSICIAN'S FINAL NOTE:

"Bitterness is discharged. Peace is permanent." The Great Physician You entered this clinic thinking it was about them. You're leaving knowing it was about you. Healing didn't happen when they changed it. It happened when you stopped needing them too. You are no longer a casualty of conflict. You are a career of calm. You are not the offended, you are the overcomer.

Your chart now reads: **Faith Stable. Forgiveness Flowing. Peace Within Normal Limits.**

✍ PATIENT SIGNATURE: _______________________
✍ PHYSICIAN SIGNATURE: _______________________
(**Holy Spirit, MD - Master of Deliverance**)

Reflections

____

____

____

____

____

____

PERSONAL NOTES

ABOUT THE AUTHOR

Dr. Patricia Tanner was born and raised in Sanford FL. She comes from a family of three siblings. Patricia Tanner is the founder of Multhai International Realty, Multhai Asset Management Services, and Multhai Investment Group which is located in Sanford, Florida. She is a graduate of the University of Central Florida, where she received a Bachelor of Science in Business Administration and a minor in Human Resources Management.

Dr. Tanner began her career shortly thereafter as a Regional Property Manager in the apartment community. Throughout her career in property management, she has built interpersonal relationships with corporate clients. She has a successful track record of increasing company revenues over $5 million annually, through hard work, commitment, creativeness, and strategic planning.

Her experience and leadership role eventually led her to achieve a Florida Real Estate Broker license. She spent fifteen years in the Real Estate field while completing a Master of Arts in Human Resources Management from Webster University, and a Master of Public Administration from Troy University. It was in this capacity that she decided to open her own brokerage company, Multhai International Realty.

In addition, Dr. Tanner finds time in her busy schedule to participate in her own Non-For-Profit Organization, Stones 2 Homes. She remains President of her organization in which she helps people build, keep, or purchase homes in affordable communities. She is the founder of PNT Property Partners in which she buys vacant land, develops it, and constructs brand new construction homes in Sanford Florida. Her overall goal is to educate and provide resources to help people overcome financial hardships and credit disadvantage to live the American Dream through homeownership in spite of economic hardship. Through her visions she will continue to grow as an entrepreneur and is willing to share her knowledge, experience, and expertise with anyone who is willing to learn.

MORE BOOKS BY THE AUTHOR

Welcome to the Faith Clinic—where your soul doesn't need to be perfect to be healed.

You've smiled through burnout. Quoted scripture while quietly unraveling. Prayed, fasted, and still felt like your faith flatlined. If that's you, Faith Clinic: Volume I is your spiritual prescription.

Dr. Patricia S. Tanner—known as The Faith Doctor—invites you into a raw, grace-filled recovery journey for the soul. With 7 powerful doses of faith-infused wisdom, this book delivers healing where performance failed and offers truth where church hurt left a scar. Designed especially for spiritually exhausted youth and young adults, each "dose" reads like an IV drip of hope for believers secretly running on empty.

You don't need to be okay to show up. You just need to be willing. The clinic is open.

NOW AVAILABLE:

www.amazon.com

Healing was just the beginning. Now it's time to grow.

If Faith Clinic Volume I met you in crisis, Volume II meets you in recovery. Because faith isn't a one-time fix—it's a lifestyle that needs maintenance, accountability, and consistency. Welcome to your follow-up care plan.

In Faith Clinic: Volume II, Dr. Patricia S. Tanner—aka The Faith Doctor—guides you through the next level of your spiritual healing journey. From navigating church trauma and burnout to facing silence from God and rediscovering purpose, this book goes deeper than devotionals. It's not about hype—it's about habits that sustain real, lasting transformation.

With raw wisdom, relatable stories, and no-shame truths, each chapter is a spiritual check-in for believers who want to thrive—not just survive. Whether you're wrestling with doubt, craving stability, or simply ready to grow up in God, this clinic is for you.

You've detoxed. Now it's time to build. Let's get you discharge-ready.

NOW AVAILABLE:

www.amazon.com

Welcome to the Faith Clinic: Anxiety Edition — where God doesn't coddle your coping mechanisms but confronts them with surgical precision.

This book is for the ones who love Jesus but still can't sleep. For the worship leaders crying in church bathrooms. For the believers who pray in spirals, fight shame on Sundays, and secretly think, "Maybe I'm the only one who can't seem to breathe through this." You're not crazy. You're just in a fight — and this book is your spiritual triage.

Inside you'll find:
- Panic attacks in pews and the prayers that still work.
- Scriptures that talk you off the ledge.
- What to do when you feel numb and God feels quiet.
- How to walk out of shame loops, judgment spirals, and performance religion.

This isn't just encouragement. It's equipment.
Because healing isn't a moment — it's a walk.

NOW AVAILABLE:

www.amazon.com

Welcome to the Faith Clinic: Stress Edition — where we don't hand you cute verses and clichés. We hand you spiritual prescriptions for real pressure, real panic, and real prayers from tired believers holding it together by a thread.

This book is for the overwhelmed—those trusting God while juggling bills, burnout, hustle culture, and holy frustration. If you've ever whispered, "God, are You even watching this mess?" this is for you.

Inside you'll find raw, soul-hitting chapters like:

- "God, I Trust You — But These Bills Keep Coming"
- "If Rest Is Holy, Why Does It Feel Like Slacking?"
- "I'm Tired of Smiling So You Won't Worry"

This isn't fluff. It's real talk for real stress—and a reminder that you're not forgotten, you're being fortified.

The Faith Clinic is open. Breathe in & take your spiritual vitamins. Healing begins here.

NOW AVAILABLE:

www.amazon.com

This isn't just a feeling — it's a flare signal from the soul. You pray, serve, and believe in God, but something deep inside is still simmering. Welcome to the Faith Clinic: Anger Edition — where suppressed emotions meet sacred intervention.

In this volume, Dr. Patricia S. Tanner guides you through spiritual triage for:

- Silent rage and emotional suppression
- The grief–anger connection
- Rejection wounds from childhood to church hurt

This isn't a lecture. It's a spiritual detox. No shame. No sugar-coating. Just raw, honest healing. Whether you're snapping at loved ones or silently seething under the surface, this book meets you at the boiling point—and leads you to the breakthrough.

This is the clinic.

This is your moment.

And God is ready to heal the anger behind your amen.

NOW AVAILABLE:

www.amazon.com

In this powerful installment of the Faith Clinic series, Dr. Patricia S. Tanner brings biblical insight, emotional compassion, and spiritual strength to those walking through grief. Designed as a healing chamber for the soul, each "dose" of this devotional targets a different dimension of sorrow—guiding you from pain to peace, from mourning to joy.

Inside, you'll discover:

- Daily doses of Scripture-based encouragement.
- Personal reflections and prayers for each stage of grief.
- Practical faith prescriptions to help you process loss and find purpose.

Whether you are navigating the recent loss of a loved one, confronting buried grief from the past, or supporting someone else in their sorrow, this devotional offers a gentle yet powerful roadmap to healing. Come, take your seat in the Faith Clinic—where the Great Physician is ready to restore your soul.

NOW AVAILABLE:

www.amazon.com

30 Days Of Grieving
Given By The Inspiration Of God
Healing From COVID-19

Almost a year later, it hit me... My mother was gone, and I was still stuck at the hospital. I had tried everything from crying to counseling, and even prayer. Pray they told me. Trust God they insisted. But it seemed as if nothing was working. I was hurt, dealing with my reality: my mother was not coming back.

While journeying through grief, it was under the divine 'Inspiration of God' that He placed me in a trance. While I was gaining a revelation about grief, He gave me this journal, '30 Days Of Grieving.'

NOW AVAILABLE:
www.amazon.com

The 30 Days Challenge:

I Tested POSITIVE for COVID-19

If you had 30 days to live, what would you do? If you were told that you needed to prepare for a marathon in 30 days and you were completely out of shape, what would you do first? If a family member handed you one million dollars and told you that you had to figure out how to build a house (debt free), how would you execute your plan?

I'm catching you off guard with these requests, right? Well, this is exactly what COVID-19 did when it snatched my mother's life away, wrecking my entire world. I had to battle for my mother AND my faith in 30 days flat. What a challenge!

Throughout this book, I will walk you through my brief journey with COVID-19, negative of a happy ending. I will share the diary I kept while attending to my mother, and the scriptures I read, prayed, and quoted as my shield and protection.

Take the journey with me, there is healing on the other side!

NOW AVAILABLE:

www.amazon.com

Can Salvation Get You Into Heaven? The Answer Is Yes! offers a powerful and biblically grounded exploration of God's eternal plan, revealing the heart of the Gospel and the assurance of salvation through Jesus Christ.

 Unpacking life's most vital questions—Who is God? Why were we created? What does Jesus' life mean for us?—this book brings clarity to the believer's journey and confirms that salvation, once received, is eternally secure.

Whether you're seeking understanding or affirming your faith, this inspiring guide will lead you into the confidence and joy of knowing heaven is your eternal home.

NOW AVAILBLE:

www.amazon.com

What happens when the Kingdom becomes a stranger?

The Godless Climb is not a rejection of faith—it is a raw, unflinching journey through what remains when belief unravels. With brutal honesty and tender grace, this book explores the spiritual free fall that follows the loss of divine certainty, the ache of unanswered prayers, and the void left when God no longer feels near.

Written for those who have quietly slipped out of the pews and into a wilderness of doubt, grief, and inner searching, this is not a triumph story—but a survival story. A confession. A sacred wrestle. Through personal reflection and prophetic insight, the author unpacks what it means to climb without a safety net, to live without the scaffolding of religious performance, and to build a new compass in the absence of old crutches.

You haven't arrived. But you're still climbing. And that is holy.

NOW AVAILABLE:

www.amazon.com

The Triple 7 Formula is designed for business owners who are looking forward to hitting the million-dollar mark in their business. If you own a business and seem to be running in financial circles, this book will get you on track to simultaneously gaining sound business structure and millions in your bank account.

It was through many conversations with business owners lacking financial gain that prompted Patricia to share her blueprint for millionaire status. Through this book, she demonstrates how to gain financial ground by developing strong teams, implementing systems, and setting stackable goals. If you are ready to gain a laser sharp focus, and implement these clear steps, you will position yourself for financial greatness. Your business will be sound, and you will see financial growth beyond your wildest dreams!!

NOW AVAILABLE:

www.amazon.com

The Triple 7 Formula is specifically crafted for business owners aspiring to reach the million-dollar milestone. If you are a business owner feeling stuck in financial cycles, this book will set you on the path to building both a solid business structure and financial success.

This workbook is designed to complement the textbook of the same name. As you progress through its pages, you will be inspired to take decisive steps toward becoming a millionaire. From constructing your business framework to creating the millionaire's avatar, this process will expand your knowledge and mindset. Not only will you chart a course to financial success, but you will also identify your accountability circle and select a mentor to guide you toward greatness.

I cannot guarantee millionaire status unless you actively follow the steps to begin your journey. If you are searching for a get rich quick scheme, this workbook is not for you. I am looking for those ready to put in the effort—and since you are reading this, I believe that's you!

You have finally found it: Your roadmap to millions!

NOW AVAILABLE:
WWW.Amazon.com

Find Patricia on The Web:

www.PatriciaTanner.com

Follow Patricia on social media:

Facebook & Instagram: @PatriciaTannerInc